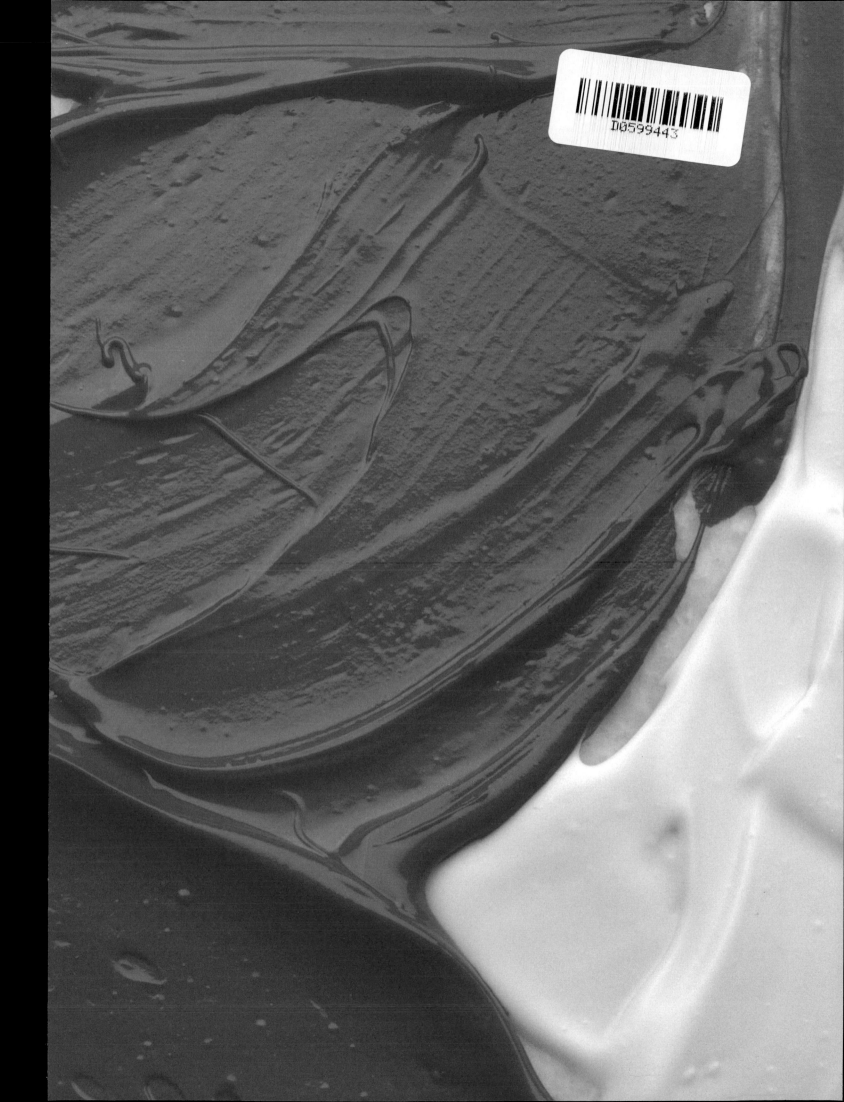

CLOSE-UP ON
CAKES

CLOSE-UP ON
CAKES

EASY RECIPES
FOR EVERY OCCASION

Edited by Suzie Smith

RIZZOLI
NEW YORK

First published in the United States of America in 1995 by
RIZZOLI INTERNATIONAL PUBLICATIONS, INC.
300 Park Avenue South, New York, NY 10010

Copyright Weldon Russell © 1995

Library of Congress Cataloging-in-Publication Data
Close up on cakes / Suzie Smith, general editor.
    p.   cm.
    Includes index.
    ISBN 0-8478-1856-X
    1. Cake.   I. Smith, Suzie
TX771.C54   1995
641.8'653—dc20   94–35428
                                       CIP

Produced by Weldon Russell Pty Ltd
107 Union Street
North Sydney, NSW 2060, Australia

Authors: Rosslyn Allert, Irma Birchell, Nicola Mappin,
  Tracey Port, Suzie Smith
Introductions: Kirsty McKenzie
Designer: Fred Rainey/Folio Art & Design
Food Stylist/General Editor: Suzie Smith
Photographer: Rowan Fotheringham

Production by South China Printing Co. (1988) Ltd.
Printed in Hong Kong

A KEVIN WELDON PRODUCTION

Opposite title page: Almond & Apricot Truffle Cake
  (page 102)
Title page: Apricot Meringue Layer Cake (page 44)
Opposite: Coconut & Raspberry Cupcakes (page 92)
Opposite contents page: Hummingbird Cake (page 104)

CONTENTS

Introduction

•

Since the time of the Egyptians, cakes have been
baked as sources of nourishment, to enliven the
daily fare, and to mark special occasions and feasts.
Little has changed in the modern world, where
a home-baked cake is still admired and relished.
Here are over 80 mouth-watering cake recipes, ranging
from traditional favorites to exciting new creations,
that will impress your family and friends and have
them coming back for more!

akes, the French philosopher Jean-Paul Sartre is alleged to have said, have faces like humans. "Spanish cakes are ascetic with a swaggering appearance, they crumble into dust under the tooth," *Larousse Gastronomique* reports him as saying. "Greek cakes are greasy, like little oil lamps: when you press them, the oil oozes out. German cakes are bulky and soft like shaving cream...But those Italian cakes have a cruel perfection: really small and flawless, scarcely bigger than *petit fours*, they gleam..."

Who knows what he would have made of the first cakes enjoyed in ancient times — a crude amalgam of maple or birch syrup, wild honey, fruits, and seeds. The Egyptian tombs of the third millennium BC provide the first evidence of baked cakes, which were placed in the pyramids to nourish the deceased on his journey to the next world. By the second century BC, the Romans were making *satura*, a mixture of barley mash, dried raisins, pine kernels, and pomegranate seeds laced with honey wine. The first-century gourmet, Apicius, described another Roman cake containing ground pepper, garam, honey, undiluted wine, rue, pine nuts, mixed boiled spelt, crushed walnuts, and toasted hazelnuts, a precursor, perhaps, of the fruitcake, which is such an important part of many modern celebrations.

One of the difficulties in tracing the history of cake is that, for many centuries, the term bread covered not only bread itself but cakes, cookies, and pastries also. However, they all owe their origin to a cornerstone of sustenance, a mixture of flour and water, which was baked to make it more palatable, and later enlivened with a whole pantry of ingredients (from eggs, sugar, and yeast to fruit, nuts, and spices) to make it actually desirable. The British coined the word "cake" in the sixteenth century, where it originally referred to a flattened sort of regularly shaped bread which was turned in baking in the manner of a Scottish oatcake. About this time, the first Christmas cakes were emerging in Germany, where bakers had been taking advantage of the spice trade and introduced ginger, cinnamon, nutmeg, almonds, rose water, and orange to their *küchen* or cakes.

The French word *gateau* comes from the Old French "wastel," meaning food. The name has evolved with the recipe through the centuries, from the original flat rounds of flour and water to the almost sculptural creations of Antonin Carême, chef to the European aristocracy of the late-eighteenth and early-nineteenth centuries. In between times, each region developed its specialty — the Artois had *gateaux razis*, the Bourbonnais, cheese tarts, and hearth cakes evolved in Normandy. During the seventeenth century, master chef François La Varenne wrote the first systematically planned cookbooks showing the distinctly French style and making public his cake formulae, including that of his famous *tourte admirable*, a marzipan base covered with lime cream, preserved cherries, and meringue. Until the seventeenth century, it was customary in Paris for wafers to be thrown on the heads of worshipers gathered in Nôtre Dame at Whitsuntide, while the Simnel cake evolved in England for Mothering Sunday. More recently, it has become synonymous with Easter, which is also when the Germans enjoy the *ostertorte*, a mocha buttercream-filled sponge decorated with chocolate eggs, and the Russians, the tower-shaped *kulich* and *pashka*.

The Italian Easter tradition of almond-based "holy lambs" dates from at least the seventeenth century, when cloistered nuns started selling them from the convents. In China, the August Moon festival is celebrated with imprinted moon cakes filled with sweet lotus seed, minced meat, or bean paste, while no Balinese temple festival would be complete

without the towering offerings of fluorocolored rice cakes.

Modern cakes can be divided into four broad categories which derive from their basic mixing methods—those that have the fat and sugar creamed, those that have the fat rubbed into the dry ingredients, varieties in which the butter is melted before the other ingredients are mixed in, and those in which eggs are whisked to give a lighter texture.

Necessity is said to have mothered the invention of many cakes—the Australian lamington is alleged to have been created when a cook was landed with some unexpected visiting dignitaries and nothing in the larder but some stale sponge and coconut. The need for economy and health consciousness is attributed to the birth of America's angel food cake, which contains neither fats nor egg yolks, while the popularity of carrot and zucchini (courgette) cakes is jointly credited to the same demand for healthier foods (oil instead of butter, increased fiber content) and the need for quick-mix and processor recipes for today's busy cooks.

Among the countless references to cakes through the ages, there are occasions when cakes have actually shaped history rather than vice versa. It is one of life's more delicious snippets of useless information that Marie Antoinette's throwaway "Let them eat cake" is firstly not what she said and secondly, not even her own line. On being told that her people had no bread, the wife of Louis XVI retorted *"Qu'il mangent de la brioche,"* [Why don't they eat brioche?] referring to the egg-enriched bread enjoyed at court, and borrowing a remark made some hundred years earlier by Marie-Therese, wife of Louis XIV. According to Rousseau's *Confessions* of 1740, the original quote was: *"Que mangent-ils de la croute de pate?"* [Why don't they eat pastry?] Who knows if the revolutionary mob might have treated their monarch more kindly if they'd known she was only jesting. Perhaps if Marie had known when to be quiet, she might even have been spared the guillotine.

Chocolate

•

The Aztecs believed cacao-tree seeds originated in paradise and brought wisdom to those who ate the plant's fruit. While there's no guarantee of enlightenment with these chocolate cakes, the connection with paradise is easy to understand.

MISSISSIPPI CHOCOLATE & COFFEE CAKE
Serves 8–10

2 cups (8 oz/250 g) all-purpose
(plain) flour
1 teaspoon baking soda
(bicarbonate of soda)
Pinch salt
1³/₄ cups (14 fl oz/440 ml)
brewed Italian coffee
¹/₄ cup (2 fl oz/60 ml) bourbon
5 oz (155 g) unsweetened chocolate
1 cup (8 oz/250 g) butter
2 cups (1 lb/500 g) sugar
2 eggs, lightly beaten
1 teaspoon vanilla extract (essence)

ICING
200 g (6¹/₂ oz) semisweet
(dark) chocolate
4¹/₂ tablespoons (2¹/₄ oz/65 g) butter

Preheat the oven to 350°F (180°C/Gas 4). Grease and line a 9-inch (23-cm) round cake pan.
In a mixing bowl, sift together the flour, baking soda, and salt.
In the top of a double boiler set over simmering water, heat the coffee, bourbon, chocolate, and butter, stirring until the chocolate and butter are melted and the mixture is smooth. Remove the pan from the heat and stir in the sugar. Let the mixture cool for 3 minutes and transfer to an electric mixer. Add the flour mixture to the chocolate mixture, half a cup at a time, and beat medium speed for 1 minute. Add the eggs and vanilla and beat until smooth.
Pour into the prepared pan and bake for 1¹/₂ hours, or until a skewer inserted in the center comes out clean. Let the cake cool completely in the pan. When cooled, turn out onto a serving plate.
Icing: Combine the chocolate and butter in the top of a double boiler and stir over low heat until they are melted and combined. Cool slightly and then ice cake.

APRICOT & RUM CHOCOLATE CAKE
Serves 8–10

¹/₂ teaspoon baking soda
(bicarbonate of soda)
¹/₂ cup (2 oz/60 g) cocoa powder
²/₃ cup (5 fl oz/155 ml) boiling water
¹/₂ cup (4 oz/125 g) sweet (unsalted) butter
1 cup (5 oz/155 g) lightly
packed brown sugar
3 eggs, separated
²/₃ cup (5 fl oz/155 ml) buttermilk
or sour cream
2 cups (8 oz/250 g)
all-purpose (plain) flour, sifted
¹/₂ cup (4 oz/125 g) sugar
3 tablespoons dark rum
Whipped cream and melted chocolate
to decorate

APRICOT FILLING
2³/₄ oz (80 g) chopped dried apricots,
soaked in 2 tablespoons dark
rum for 20 minutes
8 oz (250 g) mascarpone
¹/₃ cup (1 oz/30 g) confectioners' (icing) sugar

PREVIOUS PAGES: Mississippi Chocolate & Coffee Cake
OPPOSITE: Apricot & Rum Chocolate Cake

Preheat the oven to 350°F (180°C/Gas 4). Grease a 9-inch (23-cm) round cake pan.

Combine the baking soda, cocoa powder, and boiling water in a large bowl and stir until smooth. Let cool. Beat the butter and brown sugar until light. Add the egg yolks, one at a time, beating well after each addition. Add to the cocoa mixture. Stir in the buttermilk alternately with the flour.

Beat the egg whites until stiff peaks form. Gradually add the sugar and beat until the mixture is smooth and shiny. Fold into the cocoa mixture.

Pour the mixture into the prepared pan and bake for 1 hour, or until a skewer inserted in the center comes out clean. Let stand in the pan for 10 minutes before turning onto a wire rack to cool.

Apricot Filling: Mix all of the ingredients well. When the cake is cool, cut into 3 layers. Place the bottom layer onto a serving plate and sprinkle or brush with the rum. Spread with half of the apricot filling. Repeat for the second layer, and then top with the third layer. Spread the top layer with whipped cream and pipe on the chocolate.

CHOCOLATE CHIP CAKE

Serves 8–10

**8 oz (250 g) cream cheese,
cut into small pieces
1 cup (8 oz/250 g) sweet (unsalted)
butter, cut into small pieces
1½ cups (12 oz/375 g) sugar
5 eggs
2 tablespoons buttermilk
1 teaspoon vanilla extract (essence)
2½ cups (10 oz/315 g)
all-purpose (plain) flour
2 teaspoons baking powder
1 cup (6 oz/185 g) chocolate chips
Confectioners' (icing) sugar,
for dusting**

Preheat the oven to 350°F (180°C/Gas 4). Grease and flour a 9- x 5-inch (23- x 13-cm) loaf pan. Place the cream cheese, butter, and sugar in a food processor and process until smooth. It may be necessary to do this in 3 or 4 batches. When smooth, beat in the eggs, buttermilk, and vanilla. Sift together the flour and baking powder and fold in, along with the chocolate chips. Spoon into prepared pan and bake for 1 hour, or until a skewer inserted in the center comes out clean. Let cool for 5–10 minutes before turning out onto a wire rack to cool completely. Serve dusted with the sugar.

CHOCOLATE & NUT TORTE

Serves 8–10

**1²⁄₃ cups (6½ oz/200 g)
combined almonds and hazelnuts
8 oz (250 g) semisweet (dark)
chocolate, chopped
6 egg whites
Pinch salt
⅓ cup (3 oz/90 g)
superfine (caster) sugar
3½ oz (100 g) chopped glacéed figs
3½ oz (100 g) chopped dried dates
1¾ oz (50 g) chopped
glacéed apricots**

Preheat the oven to 350°F (180°C/Gas 4). Grease a 9-inch (23-cm) springform pan and line with foil. Place the almonds and hazelnuts, and chocolate in the bowl of a food processor and process until fine. Beat together the egg whites with a pinch of salt until almost stiff. Gradually add the sugar and continue beating until the mixture forms a meringue.

Stir in one-third of the chocolate and nut mixture and one-third of the fruit. Fold through the remaining chocolate and fruit.

Pour into prepared pan and bake for 45 minutes. After 45 minutes, turn off the oven and allow the cake to cool in the oven with the door ajar. When cooled, turn out and wrap in plastic wrap and foil and refrigerate overnight before serving.

ABOVE AND OPPOSITE: Chocolate Chip Cake
FOLLOWING PAGES: Chocolate & Nut Torte (left) and Prune & Marzipan Chocolate Marble Cake (right)

PRUNE & MARZIPAN CHOCOLATE MARBLE CAKE

Serves 8–10

1⅓ cups (8 oz/250 g) prunes, pitted and halved
¼ cup (2 fl oz/60 ml) amaretto or brandy
4 eggs
1¼ cups (10 oz/315 g) sugar
1½ cups (12 fl oz/375 ml)
light (single) cream
2 cups (8 oz/250 g)
self-rising flour, sifted
¾ cup (5 oz/155 g) chopped marzipan
¼ cup (1 oz/30 g) cocoa powder, sifted
Confectioners' (icing) sugar, for dusting

Soak the prunes in the amaretto for at least 2 hours. Grease and flour a kugelhopf pan. Preheat the oven to 300°F (150°C/Gas 2).

Beat the eggs with the sugar until pale and thick. Stir in the cream. Fold in the flour, prunes, and marzipan. Divide the mixture in half and stir the cocoa powder into one part of the batter. Place the pale mixture into the prepared pan and top with the cocoa mixture. Bake for 1–1¼ hours, or until a skewer inserted in the center comes out clean. Cool for 5 minutes in the pan, then turn out onto a wire rack to cool completely. Serve dusted with confectioners' (icing) sugar. This recipe is shown on page 19.

ABOVE AND OPPOSITE: Chocolate Orange Cake

CHOCOLATE ORANGE CAKE

Serves 8–10

6½ oz (200 g) semisweet (dark)
chocolate, chopped
1½ cups (6 oz/185 g)
all-purpose (plain) flour
1 teaspoon baking powder
2 pinches salt
¾ cup (6 oz/185 g) sweet (unsalted)
butter, at room temperature
⅔ cup (5 oz/155 g) sugar
5 eggs, separated
¾ cup (6 fl oz/185 ml)
orange marmalade (preferably bitter)
¼ cup (1 oz/30 g) ground almonds

Preheat the oven to 350°F (180°C/Gas 4). Grease and line a 9-inch (23-cm) round springform pan. Melt the chocolate in the top of a double boiler over simmering water. Remove from heat and let cool to room temperature. Sift the flour, baking powder and a pinch of salt into a bowl and set aside.

Beat the butter and sugar until light and fluffy. Add the egg yolks one at a time, beating thoroughly after each addition. Stir the cooled chocolate and ¼ cup (2 fl oz/60 ml) of the marmalade. Gradually stir in the dry ingredients. Stir in the ground almonds. The mixture will be stiff.

Beat the egg whites with the remaining pinch of salt until stiff peaks form. Fold one-third of beaten egg whites into mixture to loosen it slightly. Carefully fold in the remaining whites in 2 additions.

Spoon the mixture into the prepared pan and smooth the top with a spatula. Bake for about 1 hour, or until a skewer inserted in the center comes out clean.

Cool the cake in the pan for 5 minutes. Turn out onto a rack to cool completely.

Heat the remaining ½ cup (4 fl oz/125 ml) of marmalade in a small heavy pan over low heat, stirring constantly until melted. Brush the marmalade over the cake in several thin coats with a pastry brush. Let set for about 20 minutes at room temperature before serving.

PANFORTE

Serves 8–10

1 cup (4 oz/125 g) slivered almonds
1 cup (4 oz/125 g) coarsely
chopped roasted hazelnuts
2 oz (60 g) glacéed apricots, chopped
2 oz (60 g) glacéed orange
peel, chopped
2 oz (60 g) glacéed pineapple, chopped
2 oz (60 g) glacéed figs, chopped
5 oz (155 g) semisweet (dark)
chocolate, chopped
²⁄₃ cup (2³⁄₄ oz/80 g)
all-purpose (plain) flour
2 tablespoons cocoa powder
1 teaspoon ground cinnamon
¹⁄₃ cup (3 oz/90 g) sugar
²⁄₃ cup (5 fl oz/155 ml) honey
Confectioners' (icing) sugar

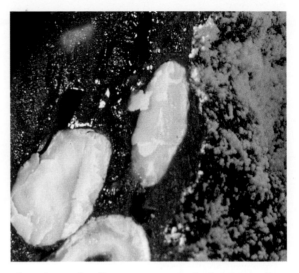

Preheat the oven to 350°F (180°C/Gas 4). Grease and line an 8-inch (20-cm) round cake pan.

Mix together the nuts, fruits, one-third of the chocolate, the flour, cocoa, and cinnamon in a bowl until combined.

Combine the remaining chocolate, the sugar, and honey in a pan and stir over low heat until melted. Bring to a boil and simmer for 1 minute. Pour the hot mixture into the fruit and nut mixture. Stir quickly to combine. Spread the mixture into the prepared pan. Bake for 35 minutes, or until firm. Cool slightly in the pan before turning onto a wire rack. Serve dusted with confectioners' (icing) sugar.

PANFORTE

1. Combine the nuts, fruits, one-third of the chocolate, the flour, cocoa, and cinnamon in a bowl.

3. Pour the hot mixture into the fruit and nut mixture. Stir quickly to combine.

2. Combine the remaining chocolate, the sugar, and honey in a pan and stir over low heat until melted.

4. Spread the mixture into the prepared pan.

OPPOSITE: Panforte

JURASSIC CHOCOLATE CAKE

Serves 8–10

2 oz (60 g) brazil nuts, halved
4 oz (125 g) chopped glacéed apricots
4 oz (125 g) chopped glacéed figs
3 oz (90 g) chopped pitted prunes
2$^{1}/_{2}$ oz (75 g) chopped glacéed ginger
$^{1}/_{4}$ cup (2 fl oz/60 ml) plus 2 tablespoons
brandy or rum
$^{1}/_{2}$ cup (4 oz/125 g) butter
9$^{1}/_{2}$ oz (300 g) semisweet (dark)
chocolate, chopped
2 eggs, separated
$^{1}/_{2}$ cup (4 oz/125 g) sugar
$^{1}/_{2}$ cup (4 oz/125 g) sour cream
1 cup (4 oz/125 g) all-purpose (plain) flour
1 teaspoon baking powder
$^{2}/_{3}$ cup (2$^{1}/_{2}$ oz/75 g) ground almonds

ICING
6$^{1}/_{2}$ oz (200 g) semisweet (dark)
chocolate, chopped
1 tablespoon vegetable oil
Silver balls, for decorating

Combine the nuts, fruits, and $^{1}/_{4}$ cup (2 fl oz/60 ml) of the brandy in a bowl and let stand for 2–3 hours. Preheat the oven to 300°F (150°C/Gas 2). Grease and line an 8-inch (20-cm) round cake pan.

Melt the butter and chocolate in a pan. Remove from heat. Stir in the extra brandy, sugar, and egg yolks, one at a time. Stir in the sour cream. Fold in the flour, baking powder, and ground almonds. Beat the egg whites until stiff. Fold the egg whites through the chocolate fruit mixture. Spread the mixture into the pan and bake for 1$^{1}/_{2}$ hours.

Icing: Combine the chocolate and oil in the top of a double boiler. Stir over simmering water until the chocolate melts. Spread the mixture over the cooled cake and decorate with silver balls.

Jurassic Chocolate Cake

CHOCOLATE, GINGER & WALNUT CAKE

Serves 8–10

¹/₄ cup (2 fl oz/60 ml)
heavy (double) cream
6¹/₂ oz (200 g) semisweet
(dark) chocolate
5¹/₂ tablespoons
(2³/₄ oz/80 g) butter
3 eggs, separated
³/₄ cup (6 oz/185 g) sugar
1 cup (4 oz/125 g) all-purpose
(plain) flour, sifted
2 teaspoons baking powder
2¹/₂ oz (75 g) chopped glacéed ginger
3 oz (90 g) chopped walnuts

ICING
1¹/₂ oz (45 g) chopped glacéed ginger
1 tablespoon rum
¹/₂ cup (3 oz/90 g) brown sugar
¹/₂ cup (4 fl oz/125 ml) heavy (double) cream
2 tablespoons (1 oz/30 g) butter
Extra chopped glacéed ginger to decorate

Preheat the oven to 350°F (180°C/Gas 4). Grease and flour a 9-inch (23-cm) springform pan. Combine the cream and chocolate in the top of a double boiler and stir over simmering water until combined. Stir in the butter and set aside to cool.

Beat the egg yolks and sugar until pale. Stir into chocolate mixture alternately with the flour, baking powder, ginger, and walnuts.

Beat the egg whites until stiff and gently fold through the mixture. Pour into the prepared pan and bake for 30–40 minutes, or until a skewer inserted in the center comes out clean. Let cool in the pan for 15–20 minutes. Turn out onto wire rack to cool completely before icing.

Icing: Soak the ginger in the rum. Combine the sugar and one-third of the cream in a saucepan. Bring to a boil and simmer for 10 minutes. Remove from heat and whisk in the butter, ginger, and rum. Refrigerate for 10 minutes. Beat the remaining cream until soft peaks form. Gently fold into the cooled mixture and spread over the cake. Decorate with the extra chopped ginger.

CHOCOLATE, GINGER & WALNUT CAKE

1. Combine the cream and chocolate in the top part of a double boiler.

2. Stir in the butter and set aside to cool.

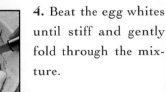

3. Beat the egg yolks and sugar until pale. Stir into the chocolate mixture alternately with the flour and baking powder, ginger, and walnuts.

4. Beat the egg whites until stiff and gently fold through the mixture.

OPPOSITE: Chocolate, Ginger & Walnut Cake

After-school Treats

After a hard day in the classroom, nourishing yet appealing cakes are in order. These recipes are quick to prepare and, in the unlikely event of leftovers, would make a welcome addition to tomorrow's lunchbox.

SCANDINAVIAN OATMEAL CAKE
Serves 10

1¼ cups (10 fl oz/315 ml) boiling water
1 cup (3 oz/90 g) rolled oats
1 cup (6 oz/185 g) packed brown sugar
1 cup (8 oz/250 g) sugar
½ cup (4 oz/125 g) butter, melted
2 eggs
1⅓ cups (5½ oz/170 g)
all-purpose (plain) flour
1½ teaspoons ground cinnamon
¾ teaspoon baking powder
½ teaspoon salt

TOPPING
½ cup (3 oz/90 g) packed brown sugar
½ cup (1½ oz/45 g) walnut halves
½ cup (¾ oz/20 g)
freshly grated or canned coconut
½ cup (4 oz/125 g) butter, melted
½ teaspoon ground cinnamon

Preheat the oven to 350°F (180°C/Gas 4). Butter a 9-inch (23-cm) springform cake pan and line with parchment or waxed (greaseproof) paper.

In a bowl pour the boiling water over the oats and stir. In another bowl combine both sugars and the melted butter. Beat in the eggs, one at a time, beating well after each addition. Stir in the oat mixture until all is well blended. Sift together the flour, cinnamon, baking powder, and salt and add to the oat mixture. Stir until blended.

Pour the batter into the prepared pan and smooth the top. Bake for 1 hour, or until a skewer inserted in the center comes out clean. Cool in the pan on a wire rack for at least 10 minutes before removing the sides of the pan.

Topping: In a bowl, combine the sugar, walnuts, coconut, butter, and cinnamon and spread over the top of the cake. Place under a preheated broiler (grill),

about 4 inches (10 cm) from the heat, for 4–5 minutes, or until the topping is golden and bubbling. Serve warm or at room temperature.

•

BANANA CAKE
Serves 8–10

4 oz (125 g) cream cheese
½ cup (4 oz/125 g) butter,
at room temperature
1 cup (6 oz/185 g) packed brown sugar
2 eggs
2 large ripe bananas, mashed
2 cups (8 oz/250 g) all-purpose (plain) flour
1 tablespoon baking powder
¼ cup (1 oz/30 g) ground almonds

ICING
8 oz (250 g) cream cheese
1 cup (6 oz/185 g) confectioners' (icing) sugar
1 large ripe banana
2 tablespoons lemon juice

Preheat the oven to 375°F (190°C/Gas 5). Butter a 4 x 8-inch (10 x 20-cm) loaf pan.

Beat the cream cheese, butter, and sugar together until creamy. Add the eggs, one at a time, beating well. Stir in the bananas, then mix in the flour, baking powder, and nuts. Spoon the mixture into the prepared pan.

Place in the oven and bake for 1 hour, or until a skewer inserted in the center comes out clean. Turn out onto a rack to cool completely.

Icing: Beat together the cream cheese and confectioners' (icing) sugar until smooth and ice the cake. Peel and thinly slice the banana. Toss the slices in the lemon juice, then arrange over the top of the icing. Serve immediately.

PREVIOUS PAGES: Scandinavian Oatmeal Cake
ABOVE AND OPPOSITE: Banana Cake

APRICOT & WALNUT LOAF

Serves 10–12

1½ cups (6 oz/185 g) dried apricots
1 cup (8 fl oz/250 ml) water
2 cups (8 oz/250 g) self-rising flour
½ teaspoon baking soda
(bicarbonate of soda)
⅔ cup (5 oz/155 g) sugar
1 teaspoon grated orange zest (rind)
¾ cup (3 oz/90 g) walnut
pieces, finely chopped
⅓ cup (3 fl oz/90 ml) orange juice
1 egg
¼ cup (2 oz/60 g) butter, melted

Preheat the oven to 300°F (150°C/Gas 2). Butter
a 4½ x 9-inch (12 x 23-cm) loaf pan and line with
parchment or waxed (greaseproof) paper.
Place the dried apricots and water in a saucepan.
Bring to a boil, then reduce the heat and simmer,
covered, for 10 minutes, or until the apricots are
tender. Drain, reserving ¼ cup (2 fl oz/60 ml) of
the liquid. Cool the apricots and roughly chop.
Sift the flour and baking soda (bicarbonate of
soda) together into a bowl. Add the sugar, orange zest (rind), walnuts, and apricots.
In a separate bowl, beat together the orange
juice, egg, melted butter, and reserved apricot
liquid. Add to the dry ingredients and mix well.
Spoon the mixture into the prepared pan and
bake for 50–60 minutes, or until a skewer inserted in the middle of the cake comes out clean.
Let cool in the pan for 5 minutes before turning
out onto a wire rack to cool completely.
Serve cut into slices.

Apricot & Walnut Loaf

HONEY CAKE
Serves 10–12

1 cup (8 fl oz/250 ml) honey
$^1/_2$ cup (4 fl oz/120 ml) black coffee
2 eggs
$^1/_2$ cup (3 oz/90 g) packed brown sugar
$^3/_4$ cup (6 fl oz/185 ml) grapeseed oil
2 cups (8 oz/250 g) self-rising flour
$^1/_2$ teaspoon baking soda
(bicarbonate of soda)
$^3/_4$ cup (6$^1/_2$ oz/200 g) mixed dried fruit
(apricots, currants or raisins), chopped
$^1/_2$ cup (3 oz/90 g) almonds, chopped
2 glacéed figs
Confectioners' (icing) sugar to decorate

Preheat the oven to 325°F (170°C/Gas 3). Butter a 9–10-inch (23–25-cm) round cake pan. Combine the honey and coffee in a small saucepan and bring to a boil, stirring occasionally; allow to cool. Beat in the eggs, sugar, and oil. Sift together the dry ingredients, then stir in the mixed dried fruit, almonds, and figs. Fold the combined honey and egg mixture into the flour mixture.

Pour into the prepared cake pan and bake for 30 minutes. Reduce the heat to 300°F (150°C/Gas 2) and cook for a further 25 minutes, or until a skewer inserted in the middle of the cake comes out clean. Cool in the pan on a

LEFT AND RIGHT:
Honey Cake

wire rack for 10 minutes. Turn out onto the wire rack to cool completely.

Dust with confectioners' (icing) sugar and serve.

•

DATE & WALNUT LOAF
Serves 10–12

1$^2/_3$ cups (8 oz/250 g) chopped dates
$^1/_2$ cup (2 oz/60 g) chopped walnuts
$^1/_2$ cup (4 oz/125 g) sugar
Pinch salt
1 tablespoon ($^3/_4$ oz/20 g) butter
1 teaspoon baking soda (bicarbonate of soda)
1 teaspoon ground allspice
1 cup (8 fl oz/250 ml) boiling water
1$^1/_2$ cups (6 oz/185 g) self-rising flour

Preheat the oven to 350°F (180°C/Gas 4). Butter a 4 x 8-inch (10 x 20-cm) loaf pan.

Place all the ingredients except for the flour in a saucepan and stir over low heat until the butter is melted. Set aside to cool. Mix in the flour, and then pour the mixture into the prepared pan.

Bake for about 45 minutes, or until a skewer inserted in the middle of the cake comes out clean. Cool in the pan on a wire rack for 10 minutes. Turn out onto a wire rack to cool completely. Serve cut in thick slices.

APPLE & PECAN NUT CAKE
Serves 8–10

2 green cooking apples, peeled
1 cup (8 oz/250 g) sugar
1¹/₂ cups (6 oz/185 g)
all-purpose (plain) flour
1 teaspoon baking soda
(bicarbonate of soda)
1 teaspoon ground cinnamon
1 teaspoon ground allspice
¹/₂ teaspoon salt
1 cup (4 oz/125 g) chopped pecans
1 egg
¹/₂ cup (4 oz/125 g) butter, melted
Confectioners' (icing) sugar, for dusting

Preheat the oven to 375°F (190°C/Gas 5). Butter an 8-inch (20-cm) square cake pan.

Cut the apples into large dice and mix with the sugar. In another bowl sift together the dry ingredients and mix in the pecans.

Beat the egg and melted butter until combined, then add to the apple mixture. Lightly fold the sifted ingredients into the apple mixture and spoon into the prepared pan.

Bake for 45–55 minutes, or until a skewer inserted in the center comes out clean. Cool in the pan for 10 minutes before turning out onto a wire rack to cool completely. Dust with sugar and serve.

PREVIOUS PAGES:
Date & Walnut Loaf
(left) and Apple &
Pecan Nut Cake
(right) LEFT AND
RIGHT: Date Cake

DATE CAKE
Serves 8–10

1 cup (5 oz/155 g) chopped dates
¹/₃ cup (1¹/₂ oz/45 g) chopped walnuts
¹/₂ cup (3 oz/90 g) packed brown sugar
2 eggs, beaten
¹/₂ cup (4 oz/125 g) butter, melted
2 teaspoons light corn syrup
or golden syrup
³/₄ cup (3 oz/90 g) self-rising flour
³/₄ cup (3¹/₂ oz/100 g) whole wheat
(wholemeal) self-rising flour
¹/₄ cup (2 fl oz/60 ml) milk

ICING
4 oz (125 g) cream cheese
6 teaspoons (1 oz/30 g) butter
1 cup (6 oz/185 g) confectioners' (icing) sugar
Walnut halves to decorate

Preheat the oven to 350°F (180°C/Gas 4). Butter an 8-inch (20-cm) springform cake pan and line with parchment or waxed (greaseproof) paper.

In a large bowl combine all the cake ingredients and mix until combined. Pour the mixture into the prepared pan and bake for 50 minutes, or until a skewer inserted in the middle of the cake comes out clean. Cool for 10 minutes in the pan before removing the sides of the pan.

Icing: Combine all the icing ingredients and mix until smooth. Spread over the top of the cooled cake. Decorate with the walnuts and serve.

ZUCCHINI, PEACH & CAROB CAKE

Serves 8–10

3 eggs
2 cups (1 lb/500 g) sugar
2 teaspoons vanilla extract (essence)
1 cup (8 fl oz/250 ml) grapeseed oil
3 cups (12 oz/375 g) self-rising flour
2 teaspoons ground cinnamon
1½ cups (8 oz/250 g) grated
zucchini (courgette)
1 cup (4½ oz/140 g) carob
swirls or chips
1 cup (4 oz/125 g) chopped, well-drained
canned peaches

CAROB CREAM CHEESE ICING
¼ cup (2 oz/60 g) butter
4 oz (125 g) cream cheese
4 oz (125 g) carob chips, melted
and cooled slightly

Preheat the oven to 300°F (150°C/Gas 2). Lightly grease a 9-inch (23-cm) square cake pan and line with waxed (greaseproof) paper.

Beat the eggs in a bowl until frothy. Add the sugar, vanilla, and oil and beat until thick, about 3 minutes. Sift the flour and cinnamon into the mixture and stir until well combined. Stir in the zucchini (courgette), carob and peaches.

Pour the mixture into the prepared pan and bake for 1 hour. Increase the temperature to 350°F (180°C/Gas 4) and bake for a further 15–20 minutes, or until a skewer inserted in the middle of the cake comes out clean. Cool the cake in the pan for 10 minutes before turning out onto a wire rack to cool completely.

Carob Cream Cheese Icing: Beat the butter and cream cheese until light and creamy. Add the carob and beat until smooth. Spread the carob cream cheese icing over the top of the cooled cake and serve immediately.

OPPOSITE: Zucchini, Peach & Carob Cake

ZUCCHINI, PEACH & CAROB CAKE

1. Beat the eggs until frothy. Beat in the sugar.

3. Sift the flour and cinnamon into mixture and stir to combine.

2. Beat in the oil.

4. Stir in the zucchini (courgette), carob, and peaches.

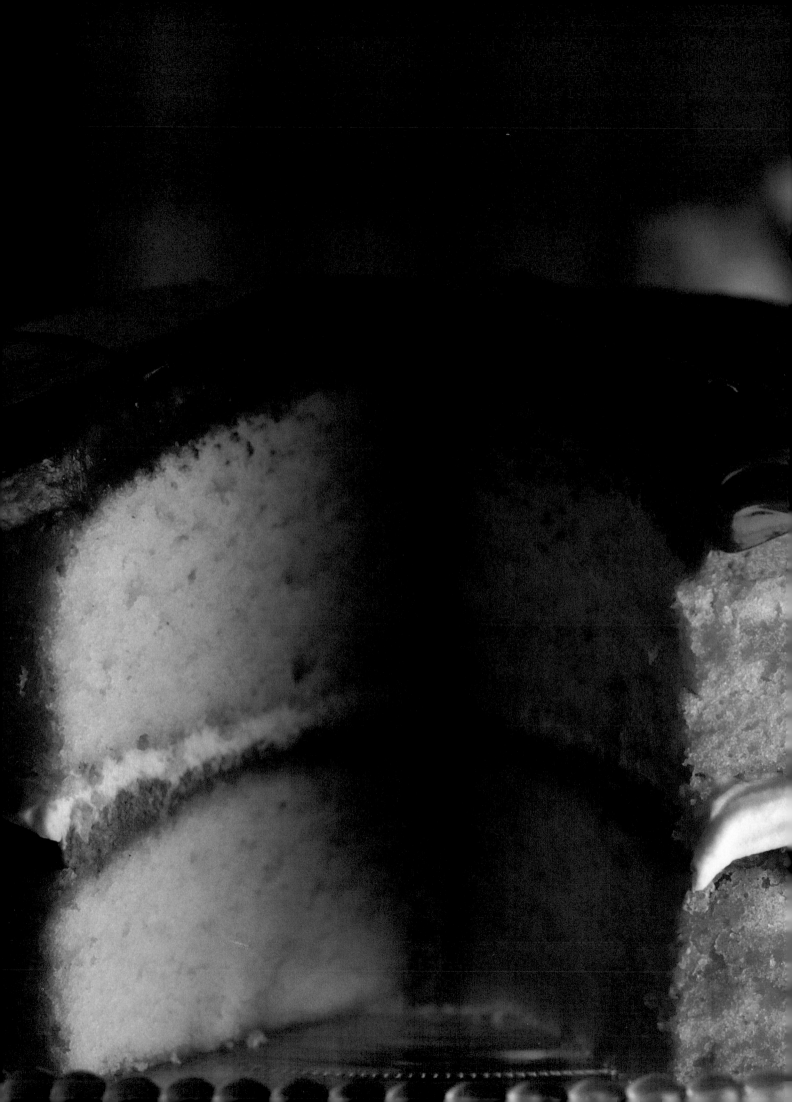

Dessert Cakes

•

When something special is called for to wrap
up a dinner party, an eye-catching, mouth-watering
cake is the ultimate prepare-ahead dessert.
The "impress-a-guest" offering is simply brought to
the table and served.

CHOCOLATE & CHESTNUT DESSERT CAKE
Serves 10–12

CAKE
2 cups (1 lb/500 g) sugar

4 eggs

1 cup (8 fl oz/250 ml)
light olive oil or sunflower oil

1 cup (8 fl oz/250 ml) dry white wine

2¹/₂ cups (10 oz/300 g)
all-purpose (plain) flour

2 teaspoons baking powder

¹/₂ teaspoon salt

CHESTNUT FILLING
14 oz (440 g) canned chestnuts, drained

¹/₄ cup (1³/₄ oz/50 g) packed brown sugar

²/₃ cup (5 fl oz/155 ml)
heavy (double) cream

GANACHE
6 oz (185 g) semisweet (dark) chocolate

³/₄ cup (6 oz/185 g) sweet (unsalted) butter

Preheat the oven to 350°F (180°C/Gas 4). Butter two 9-inch (23-cm) springform or round cake pans and line with waxed (greaseproof) paper.
Cake: Beat together the sugar and eggs to combine. Add the oil, wine, flour, baking powder, and salt and beat for 1 minute, or until smooth. Pour the mixture into the prepared pans and bake for 30 minutes, or until a skewer inserted in the middle of each cake comes out clean. Allow the cakes to cool slightly in the pans before turning out onto a wire rack to cool completely.
Chestnut Filling: Combine all of the ingredients in the bowl of a food processor

and process until smooth. Spread a layer of chestnut filling on top of each cake.
Ganache: Melt the chocolate in a double boiler, then stir in the butter. Remove from the heat and cool or refrigerate to thicken slightly. If a thicker consistency is desired, whisk gently until pale and thick, 2–3 minutes.
Spread a layer of ganache over the top of the chestnut filling on the first layer. Top with the second layer and repeat the process.
Serve the cake cut in wedges.

•

APRICOT MERINGUE LAYER CAKE
Serves 10–12

6 egg whites

1¹/₂ cups (11 oz/345 g)
superfine (caster) sugar

1¹/₂ teaspoons vanilla extract (essence)

1¹/₂ teaspoons white vinegar

1 cup (3¹/₂ oz/100 g) ground almonds

APRICOT FILLING
1²/₃ cups (6¹/₂ oz/200 g)
chopped dried apricots

1 cup (8 fl oz/250 ml) water

¹/₂ cup (4 oz/125 g) sugar

2 tablespoons (1 oz/30 g) butter

1¹/₄ cups (10 fl oz/315 ml)
heavy (double) cream, whipped

Preheat the oven to 275°F (140°C/Gas 1). Line 3 baking sheets with parchment (baking paper) and draw a 9-inch (23-cm) circle on each sheet.
Vigorously beat the egg whites until soft peaks form.

ABOVE AND OPPOSITE: Apricot Meringue Layer Cake   PREVIOUS PAGES: Chocolate & Chestnut Dessert Cake

Gradually add the sugar and beat until thick and glossy and all of the sugar is dissolved. Fold in the vanilla, vinegar, and almonds.

Divide the meringue mixture evenly among the baking sheets, spreading it on the circles. Smooth with a spatula. Bake in the oven for 45 minutes, or until each one sounds hollow when tapped lightly. Turn off the oven, cool the meringues in the oven until completely cool to touch.

Apricot Filling: Place the apricots, water, and sugar in a saucepan. Stir over a medium heat until the sugar is dissolved, then simmer for 5 minutes, or until the apricots are tender and most of the liquid is absorbed. Transfer the mixture to a food processor and process until smooth. Add the butter and process until smooth.

Place one meringue disk on a serving plate, spread with half of the apricot filling, then with half of the whipped cream. Top with another meringue disk, repeat with the remaining apricot filling and cream. Finally, top with the remaining meringue disk and serve.

FLORENTINE CHEESECAKE
Serves 10–12

CRUST
1¹/₂ cups (6 oz/185 g) Graham cracker or
shortbread crumbs
1 tablespoon brown sugar
1 tablespoon ground cinnamon
¹/₄ cup (2 oz/60 g) sweet (unsalted)
butter, melted and cooled

FILLING
1 lb (500 g) cream cheese
1 cup (8 oz/250 g) ricotta cheese
4 eggs
¹/₃ cup (1¹/₂ oz/45 g)
unsweetened cocoa powder
1 teaspoon vanilla extract (essence)
1 cup (8 oz/250 g) sugar
3 tablespoons brewed strong black coffee
2 teaspoons ground cinnamon

TOPPING
1 cup (8 fl oz/250 ml) sour cream
¹/₂ cup (4 oz/125 g) superfine (caster) sugar
1 tablespoon cocoa powder
1 teaspoon cinnamon

Line a 9-inch (23-cm) springform cake pan with foil and lightly grease the sides.

Crust: Combine the cracker or shortbread crumbs, brown sugar, and cinnamon in a bowl, then stir in the melted butter. Press the mixture into the base of the prepared pan.

Preheat the oven to 325°F (170°C/Gas 3).

Filling: Place the cream cheese, ricotta cheese, eggs, cocoa powder, and vanilla in a food processor and process until smooth. Add the sugar, coffee, and cinnamon and continue to beat for 10 minutes, or until the mixture is combined.

Pour into the crust-lined pan and bake for 1 hour, or until just firm to touch. Allow the cake to stand for 5 minutes before spreading on the topping.

Topping: Combine the sour cream, sugar, cocoa

powder, and cinnamon in a bowl and stir thoroughly. Spread over the cooked cheesecake and return to the oven for 10–15 minutes, or until just set. Allow the cheesecake to cool completely in the pan before refrigerating overnight.

To serve, run a knife around the edge of the pan and gently remove the sides.

•

ORANGE & ALMOND DESSERT CAKE
Serves 10

2 whole oranges, washed
6 eggs
1 cup (8 oz/250 g) sugar
2 cups (7 oz/220 g) freshly ground almonds
1 teaspoon baking powder
Confectioners' (icing) sugar or thin
strips of orange zest (rind), for serving

Preheat the oven to 350°F (180°C/Gas 4). Butter a 9-inch (23-cm) springform cake pan and line with parchment or waxed (greaseproof) paper. Place the oranges in a saucepan, cover with boiling water and cook for 2 hours, topping up the water as it gets low. Alternatively, microwave the halved, unpeeled oranges for 15 minutes on high. The seeds may be removed by splitting the oranges. Place the cooked, unpeeled oranges in a food processor and process until smooth.

Whisk the eggs in a large bowl. Add the sugar, ground almonds, and baking powder and stir to combine. Add the orange purée, then stir to combine thoroughly.

Pour the mixture into the prepared cake pan. Bake for 1–1¹/₄ hours, or until the cake feels firm to the touch and a skewer inserted in the middle comes out moist but not wet. Cool in the pan on a wire rack for at least 30 minutes before turning out.

Serve dusted with confectioners' (icing) sugar or decorated with orange zest (rind).

OPPOSITE: Florentine Cheesecake

SICILIAN DESSERT CAKE
Serves 10

CAKE
$^1/_2$ cup (4 oz/125 g) butter
$^1/_2$ cup (4 oz/125 g) sugar
2 eggs
1 teaspoon vanilla extract (essence)
$1^1/_4$ cups (5 oz/155 g) self-rising flour
$^1/_4$ cup (1 oz/30 g) all-purpose (plain) flour
$^1/_4$ teaspoon salt
$^1/_2$ cup (4 fl oz/125 ml) milk

FILLING
1 cup (8 oz/250 g) ricotta cheese
$^3/_4$ cup (6 fl oz/185 ml) cream
$^1/_4$ cup (2 oz/60 g) sugar
2 tablespoons chopped glacéed cherries
1 tablespoon chopped candied citrus peel
1 tablespoon chopped glacéed pineapple
1 tablespoon chopped glacéed apricots
Grated zest (rind) of $^1/_2$ orange
2 oz (60 g) semisweet (dark)
chocolate, chopped
2 tablespoons Cointreau
or other orange liqueur

ICING
4 oz (125 g) semisweet (dark) chocolate
2 tablespoons brewed strong black coffee
$^1/_3$ cup (3 oz/90 g) sweet (unsalted)
butter, cut into small pieces

Preheat the oven to 350°F (180°C/Gas 4). Butter a 9 x 5-inch (23 x 13-cm) loaf pan and line with parchment or waxed (greaseproof) paper.
Cake: Cream the butter and sugar until light and fluffy. Whisk the eggs with the vanilla. Combine with the butter mixture, stirring well. Sift together the flours and salt and fold into the butter mixture alternately with the milk.

PREVIOUS PAGES: Orange & Almond Dessert Cake (left) and Sicilian Dessert Cake (right)

Pour the batter into the prepared pan and bake for 40 minutes, or until a skewer inserted in the middle of the cake comes out clean. Turn out onto a wire rack and cool completely, preferably overnight.
If the top of the cake is not flat, trim away any domed part until the top is flat. Cut the cake horizontally into 4 layers.
Filling: Place the ricotta cheese in the bowl of a food processor and process until smooth. Add the cream and sugar and process until well combined. Transfer to a bowl and fold in all the other ingredients, except the Cointreau.
Line the cake pan with an overhanging piece of parchment or waxed (greaseproof) paper. Place the bottom layer of cake back in the pan and brush with a little of the Cointreau. Cover with one-third of the ricotta filling. Top with the next layer of cake and repeat until the remaining Cointreau, ricotta filling, and 2 layers of cake have been used, ending with a layer of cake.
Refrigerate for at least 1 hour.
Icing: Place the chocolate in a double boiler with the coffee. Stir until melted. Add the butter and stir until smooth. Remove from the heat and refrigerate for 15 minutes, or until the chocolate cools to a spreading consistency. Gently remove the cake from the pan and spread with the chocolate icing.
Serve immediately or refrigerate overnight until ready to serve.

ABOVE AND OPPOSITE: Rhubarb & Sour Cream Cake

RHUBARB & SOUR CREAM CAKE

Serves 10–12

$^1/_4$ cup (2 oz/60 g) sweet (unsalted) butter, at room temperature
$1^1/_2$ cups (8 oz/250 g) lightly packed brown sugar
1 egg, lightly beaten
1 teaspoon vanilla extract (essence)
$1^1/_2$ cups (6 oz/185 g) all-purpose (plain) flour, sifted
1 teaspoon baking powder
1 cup (8 fl oz/250 ml) sour cream
4 cups (15 oz/470 g) sliced rhubarb ($^1/_2$-inch/1-cm pieces)
$^1/_3$ cup (3 oz/90 g) superfine (caster) sugar

$^1/_2$ teaspoon freshly grated nutmeg
Heavy (double) cream, for serving

Preheat the oven to 375°F (190°C/Gas 5). Butter an 8 x 10-inch (20 x 25-cm) loaf pan and line with parchment or waxed (greaseproof) paper.

Cream the butter and sugar until fluffy, about 3–4 minutes. Beat in the egg and vanilla. Fold in the flour and baking powder alternately with the sour cream and rhubarb.

Pour the mixture into the prepared pan. Combine the sugar and nutmeg and sprinkle over the cake mixture.

Bake for 40 minutes, or until a skewer inserted in the middle of the cake comes out clean. Allow the cake to cool in the pan for 30 minutes before turning out.

Serve warm with heavy (double) cream.

APPLE BRIOCHE CAKE

Serves 10

**1 cup (8 oz/250 g)
sweet (unsalted) butter
4 lb (2 kg) green apples, peeled, cored
and cut into 1-inch (2.5-cm) cubes
2 tablespoons lemon juice
1 vanilla bean, split
³/₄ cup (6 oz/185 g) sugar
3 tablespoons Calvados or brandy
2 (1³/₄ lb/800 g) brioche loaves, cut into
slices ¹/₂-inch (1-cm) thick
with crusts removed
Heavy (double) cream, for serving**

Melt ¹/₂ cup (4 oz/125 g) of the butter in a large saucepan. Add the apples, lemon juice, vanilla bean, sugar, and Calvados or brandy. Cook over a medium–low heat for 35 minutes, or until the apples are soft and most of the liquid is absorbed. Remove from the heat and discard the vanilla bean. Allow to cool completely.

Preheat the oven to 400°F (200°C/Gas 6). Butter a 6-inch (15-cm) charlotte mold.

Melt the remaining ¹/₂ cup (4 oz/125 g) of butter in a saucepan. Fan 6–7 slices of brioche evenly in a full circle on the countertop. Place the charlotte mold on top and trim the brioche to the base size using a serrated knife. Butter both sides of each slice of brioche. Reserving 4 slices of brioche for the top, line the mold with the slices, overlapping the edges slightly, like shingles. Fill with the apple mixture and fit the remaining brioche slices on top. Chill in the refrigerator for 15 minutes. Remove the cake from the refrigerator, then bake for 30–40 minutes, or until the brioche on top is golden. Allow to cool for at least 30 minutes before serving.

Slice the cake into wedges and serve with heavy (double) cream.

APPLE BRIOCHE CAKE

1. Melt half the butter in a large saucepan. Add the apples, lemon juice, vanilla, sugar, and brandy.

3. Brush both sides of brioche with melted butter and fit into base of mold. Fan remaining buttered brioche around edges.

2. Fan 6-7 slices of brioche evenly in a full circle. Place the charlotte mold on top and trim to base size using a serrated knife.

4. Fill with apple mixture and fit remaining brioche on top.

OPPOSITE: Apple Brioche Cake

COCONUT SAVARIN
Serves 8–10

SAVARIN
1 envelope ($^1\!/_4$ oz/7 g) active dry yeast
$^1\!/_4$ cup (2 fl oz/60 ml) warm water
$^1\!/_4$ cup (2 oz/60 g) sugar
1 cup (4 oz/125 g) all-purpose (plain) flour
$^1\!/_3$ cup (1 oz/30 g) flaked (desiccated) coconut
$^1\!/_4$ cup (2 oz/60 g) butter, melted
2 eggs, lightly beaten

SYRUP
1 cup (8 oz/250 g) sugar
1 cup (8 fl oz/250 ml) water
3 cups (12 oz/375 g) sliced fresh peaches,
plums, nectarines, or apricots
$^1\!/_4$ cup (3 oz/90 g) apricot preserves
$^1\!/_2$ cup (4 fl oz/125 ml) brandy

Preheat the oven to 400°F (200°C/Gas 6). Butter a 9-inch (23-cm) savarin or ring mold.

Savarin: Dissolve the yeast in the warm water. Stir in a pinch of the sugar, then set aside in a warm place to proof.

Combine the flour, coconut, and sugar in a bowl. Make a well in the center and add the yeast mixture, butter, and eggs. Mix until combined. Cover with a damp cloth and stand in a warm place until dough has doubled in size, 20–30 minutes.

Press the dough into the prepared savarin mold. Bake for 5 minutes, then reduce the heat to 350°F (180°C/Gas 4) and bake for a further 15 minutes, or until the savarin feels firm. Turn out onto a rack and place over a tray. Pierce all over with a skewer.

Syrup: Place the sugar and water in a saucepan. Boil for 5 minutes, then reduce heat to a simmer. Using a slotted spoon, blanch the fruit in the syrup for about 1 minute. Lift out the fruit to drain and set aside. Strain the syrup through a sieve. Add the apricot preserves and brandy and reheat. Pour the hot syrup over the savarin. Arrange the poached fruit in the center of the savarin and serve.

Coconut Savarin

Quick & Easy

•

If you can't stand the heat, get out of the kitchen
as fast as you can by way of quick-mix, quick-bake
cakes which make the most of kitchen gems, such as
food processors and mixing wands.

LEMON LAYER CAKE
Serves 4

4 eggs
¹/₂ cup (4 oz/125 g) sugar
1 cup (4 oz/125 g)
all-purpose (plain) flour, sifted
4 tablespoons
(2 oz/60 g) butter, melted
1 tablespoon lemon zest (rind)
1–2 tablespoons lemon juice
Whipped cream, to serve

Preheat the oven to 350°F (180°C/Gas 4). Grease and line a 9-inch (23-cm) round cake pan.

Beat together the eggs and sugar until thick and pale and the mixture forms a ribbon. Fold in the sifted flour in 3 batches, adding the combined butter, lemon zest and lemon juice with the last batch.

Pour into the prepared pan. Bake for 25–30 minutes, or until a skewer inserted in the center comes out clean.

Let cool in the pan for 5 minutes before turning out onto a wire rack to cool completely.

Cut the cake in half to form 2 semicircles. Spread one half with the whipped cream and top with the other. Cut into wedges to serve.

PREVIOUS PAGES: Lemon Layer Cake
BELOW AND OPPOSITE: Lemon & Caraway Cake

LEMON & CARAWAY CAKE
Serves 10–12

¹/₂ cup plus 1 tablespoon (4¹/₂ oz/140 g)
sweet (unsalted) butter
1 cup (8 oz/250 g) sugar
2 eggs, separated
2 cups (8 oz/250 g) all-purpose (plain) flour
1 teaspoon baking powder
²/₃ cup (5 fl oz/155 ml) milk
2 tablespoons grated lemon zest (rind) or
¹/₂ cup (3 oz/90 g) glacéed lemon peel
1 tablespoon caraway seeds
1 teaspoon vanilla extract (essence)

Preheat the oven to 350°F (180°C/Gas 4). Butter a 4 x 8 inch (10 x 20 cm) loaf pan and line it with parchment or waxed (greaseproof) paper.

Cream the butter and sugar until light and fluffy. Add the egg yolks, one at a time, beating well after each addition. Sift together the flour and baking powder and fold into the mixture alternately with the milk, lemon zest (rind), caraway seeds, and vanilla. Beat the egg whites until stiff, then fold into the mixture.

Pour the mixture into the prepared pan. Bake for 1¹/₄ hours, or until a skewer inserted in the middle of the cake comes out clean. Allow the cake to cool in the pan on a rack for 5 minutes before turning out onto a wire rack. Serve warm or cold.

APRICOT BRANDY POUND CAKE

Serves 10–12

1 cup (8 oz/250 g) sweet (unsalted) butter
3³/₄ cups (1¹/₂ lb/750 g) sugar
6 eggs
1 cup (8 fl oz/250 ml) sour cream
¹/₂ cup (4 fl oz/125 ml) apricot brandy
1 teaspoon vanilla extract (essence)
¹/₂ cup (2 oz/60 g) chopped dried apricots
2³/₄ cups plus 1 tablespoon (11 oz/350 g)
all-purpose (plain) flour, sifted
¹/₂ teaspoon salt
¹/₄ teaspoon baking powder
¹/₄ teaspoon baking soda
(bicarbonate of soda)

ICING
1¹/₂ cups (9 oz/280 g) confectioners'
(icing) sugar
¹/₂ teaspoon sweet (unsalted) butter
1 tablespoon lemon juice
1 drop red food coloring
1 drop yellow food coloring
2 oz (60 g) dried apricots, chopped

Preheat the oven to 325°F (170°C/Gas 3). Butter and line a 9-inch (23-cm) round cake pan.
Cream the butter and sugar until light and fluffy. Add the eggs, one at a time, beating well after each addition. Beat in the sour cream, brandy, and vanilla. Stir in the apricots. Fold in the flour, salt, baking powder, and baking soda (bicarbonate of soda). Pour the mixture into the prepared pan. Bake for 1 hour, or until a skewer inserted in the middle of the cake comes out clean. Cool in the pan for 5 minutes before turning onto a rack to cool completely.
Icing: Sift the confectioners' (icing) sugar into a small bowl, stir in the butter and enough lemon juice to make a stiff paste. Stir over hot water until the icing is spreadable. Stir in the food coloring. Spread icing over cake and decorate with apricots.

Apricot Brandy Pound Cake

APPLE & POPPY SEED CAKE

Serves 8–10

²/₃ cup (5 oz/155 g) butter
1 cup (8 oz/250 g) plus 1 teaspoon sugar
3 eggs
2 cups (8 oz/250 g) self-rising flour
¹/₂ cup (2 oz/60 g)
all-purpose (plain) flour
²/₃ cup (5 fl oz/155 ml) milk
¹/₂ cup (2³/₄ oz/80 g) poppy seeds
1 tablespoon finely grated
lemon zest (rind)
2 Granny Smith apples, peeled, cored,
and very thinly sliced

Preheat the oven to 350°F (180°C/Gas 4). Butter a deep 9-inch (23-cm) round cake pan and line with parchment or waxed (greaseproof) paper.

Beat the butter and 1 cup (8 oz/250 g) of the sugar in a bowl until just combined. Add the eggs, flours, milk, poppy seeds, and lemon zest (rind). Beat the mixture on low speed with an electric mixer until combined. Then beat on high speed until the mixture is light and creamy, about 5 minutes.

Spread the mixture into the prepared pan. Arrange the apple slices, overlapping around the top of the cake, and sprinkle with the remaining 1 tea-spoon of sugar.

Bake the mixture in the oven for 45 minutes, or until a skewer inserted in the middle of the cake comes out clean. Take the cake out of the oven and let stand in the pan for 5 minutes before turning out onto a wire rack.

Serve warm or cold.

Hint: Cut the apples as thinly as possible, other-wise the apple will sink into the middle of the cake during cooking.

ABOVE AND OPPOSITE: Apple & Poppy Seed Cake

PECAN & SOUR CREAM CAKE

Serves 8–10

$^3/_4$ cup plus 1 tablespoon
($6^1/_2$ oz/200 g) sugar
$^2/_3$ cup (5 oz/155 g) butter,
chopped into small pieces
1 teaspoon vanilla extract (essence)
2 eggs
4 oz (125 g) ground almonds
1 cup (4 oz/125 g) self-rising flour
$^1/_2$ teaspoon baking soda
(bicarbonate of soda)
$^3/_4$ cup plus 1 tablespoon
($6^1/_2$ fl oz/200 ml)
sour cream or crème fraîche
$1^1/_4$ cups (5 oz/155 g) chopped pecans
1 teaspoon ground cinnamon
2 tablespoons (1 oz/30 g)
light brown sugar
Melted butter, for glazing, if desired

Preheat the oven to 350°F (180°C/Gas 4). Butter a 9-inch (23-cm) springform pan.

In a food processor, combine the sugar, chopped butter, vanilla, eggs, ground almonds, flour, baking soda (bicarbonate of soda), and sour cream. Process for 1–2 minutes, until the mixture is smooth.

Pour half of the batter into the prepared pan. Combine the pecans, cinnamon, and brown sugar and sprinkle half over the mixture in the pan. Top with the second half of the cake mixture and sprinkle with the remaining pecan, cinnamon, and sugar combination.

Bake for 1 hour, or until a skewer inserted in the middle of the cake comes out clean. Cool in the pan on a rack for 10–15 minutes. Turn out onto a wire rack to cool completely. If desired, brush the cake with the melted butter. Serve.

Pecan & Sour Cream Cake (left) and
Orange & Lemon Cake (right)

ORANGE & LEMON CAKE

Serves 8–10

1 cup (3 oz/90 g) shredded coconut
4 eggs
1 cup (8 oz/250 g) sugar
$^1/_2$ cup (4 fl oz/125 ml)
melted butter
$^3/_4$ cup plus 1 tablespoon
($3^1/_2$ oz /100 g) slivered almonds
Grated zest (rind) of 1 lemon
Grated zest (rind) of 1 orange
$^1/_2$ cup (4 fl oz/125 ml) lemon juice
$^1/_2$ cup (4 fl oz/125 ml) orange juice
1 cup (8 fl oz/250 ml) milk
$^1/_2$ cup (2 oz/60 g)
all-purpose (plain) flour

Preheat the oven to 350°F (180°C/Gas 4). Butter a 9-inch (23-cm) springform pan.

Place all the ingredients in a food processor and process until well combined, 50–60 seconds.

Pour the mixture into the prepared cake pan.

Place the pan in the oven and bake for 1 hour, or until golden brown on top and a skewer inserted in the middle of the cake comes out clean. Remove from oven, cool in the pan on a wire rack, then turn out.

This cake can be served with cream, if desired.

CHOCOLATE & PEAR BROWNIE CAKE

Serves 8–10

1 cup (8 oz/250 g) butter, melted
2 cups (1 lb/500 g) sugar
4 eggs
$^1/_2$ cup (2 oz/60 g) unsweetened
cocoa powder
2 teaspoons vanilla extract (essence)
$^3/_4$ cup (3 oz/90 g) all-purpose (plain) flour
$6^1/_2$ oz (200 g) semisweet
(dark) chocolate, chopped
$^3/_4$ cup (3 oz/90 g) chopped walnuts
1 can ($13^1/_2$ oz/425 g) pear halves, drained
10 walnut halves (optional)

Preheat the oven to 350°F (180°C/Gas 4). Lightly butter an 8-inch (20-cm) round cake pan and line with parchment or waxed (greaseproof) paper.

Mix together the melted butter, sugar, eggs, cocoa, vanilla, and flour. Stir in the chocolate and chopped walnuts, mixing well.

Pour the mixture into the prepared pan. Arrange the pears, cut sides down, on top of the mixture. Place the walnut halves between the pears, if using. Bake for 40 minutes, or until a skewer inserted in the middle of the cake comes out clean. Cool in the pan on a wire rack before turning out and serving. This cake can be served warm or cold.

ABOVE AND OPPOSITE: Chocolate & Pear Brownie Cake

FINANCIERS
Makes 12

**¾ cup plus 2 tablespoons
(4½ oz/140 g) whole almonds,
skins removed
1½ cups (9 oz/280 g)
confectioners' (icing) sugar
½ cup (2 oz/60 g)
all-purpose (plain) flour, sifted
5 egg whites
¾ cup (6 oz/185 g)
sweet (unsalted) butter,
melted and cooled
2–3 poached or canned
pear halves, thinly sliced**

Preheat the oven to 450°F (230°C/Gas 8). Butter one 12-muffin capacity, medium-sized muffin pan.

Toast the almonds on a baking sheet until golden, 5–7 minutes. Remove from the oven and cool. Place the whole almonds in a food processor and process until fine.

Combine the ground almonds with the sugar and flour in a bowl. Stir in the egg whites and mix until well blended. Add the melted butter and stir to combine thoroughly.

Spoon the mixture into the prepared muffin pans filling them three-fourths full. Lay a few slices of pear on top of each.

Bake for 15–20 minutes, or until each cake is peaked and golden and a skewer inserted in the middle comes out clean.

Turn off the oven and let the cakes remain inside with the door slightly ajar for 5 minutes. Cool in the pans for 5 minutes before turning out onto a wire rack to cool completely.

Serve warm or cold.

FINANCIERS

1. Lightly toast the almonds on a baking sheet until they are golden.

3. Add the melted butter and stir to combine thoroughly.

2. Combine the ground almonds with the sugar and flour. Stir in the egg whites until well blended.

4. Spoon the mixture into the prepared muffin molds so they are three-fourths full. Decorate with the slices of pear.

OPPOSITE: Financiers

Coffee Break

·

Whether your guests are formally invited or
spur-of-the-moment drop-ins, a cup of coffee calls for
a flavor-packed accompaniment. These cakes keep
well, and having one on hand will lend a sense of
occasion to even the solo coffee break.

CARROT CAKE
Serves 10

2 eggs
1 cup (8 oz/250 g) sugar
$^{3}/_{4}$ cup (6 fl oz/185 ml) grapeseed oil
$^{1}/_{2}$ teaspoon
vanilla extract (essence)
1 cup (4 oz/125 g) all-purpose
(plain) flour, sifted
1 teaspoon baking soda
(bicarbonate of soda)
$^{1}/_{2}$ teaspoon ground allspice
$^{1}/_{2}$ teaspoon salt
2 medium carrots, finely grated
$^{1}/_{2}$ cup (2 oz/60 g) chopped walnuts

ICING
2 tablespoons (1 oz/30 g) softened butter
2 oz (60 g) cream cheese
1 tablespoon
grated lemon zest (rind)
$1^{1}/_{2}$ cups (8 oz/250 g)
confectioners' (icing) sugar, sifted

Preheat the oven to 350°F (180°C/Gas 4). Butter an 8-inch (20-cm) loaf or ring pan.

Combine the eggs, sugar, oil, vanilla, and all the dry ingredients in a bowl, then beat until it is a smooth consistency. Stir in the carrots and walnuts. Pour the mixture into the prepared pan. Bake for 45–50 minutes, or until a skewer inserted in the middle of the cake comes out clean. Turn the cake out onto a wire rack to cool completely.

Icing: Beat the butter and cream cheese together until creamy. Mix in the lemon zest (rind) and sugar and beat until smooth.

Cover the cooled cake with the icing and serve immediately.

PREVIOUS PAGES: Carrot Cake
OPPOSITE: Poppy Seed & Hazelnut Kugelhopf

POPPY SEED & HAZELNUT KUGELHOPF
Serves 10–12

$^{3}/_{4}$ cup (6 fl oz/185 ml) milk
1 envelope ($^{1}/_{4}$ oz/7 g) active dry yeast
3 cups (12 oz/375 g)
all-purpose (plain) flour
Pinch of salt
$^{1}/_{4}$ cup (2 oz/60 g) sugar
3 eggs, lightly beaten
$^{1}/_{2}$ cup (4 oz/125 g) butter, melted
$^{1}/_{2}$ cup ($1^{3}/_{4}$ oz/50 g) poppy seeds
$^{1}/_{4}$ cup (2 fl oz/60 ml) milk
$^{1}/_{2}$ cup (2 oz/60 g) ground hazelnuts
Grated zest (rind) of 3 oranges
$^{1}/_{4}$ cup (2 fl oz/60 ml) orange juice
Confectioners' (icing) sugar, for dusting

Generously butter an 8-inch (20-cm) fluted Kugelhopf mold or bundt pan.

Heat the milk to body temperature (100°F/37°C), then pour onto the yeast and stir until dissolved. Sift the flour and salt into a warmed bowl, making a well in the center. Add the yeast mixture, sugar, eggs, and butter and beat well. Divide the mixture into 3 equal portions. To the first portion, add the poppy seeds and 2 tablespoons (1 fl oz/30 ml) of the milk. Mix well, ensuring that the poppy seeds are evenly distributed throughout the dough. To the second portion, add the hazelnuts and the remaining 2 tablespoons (1 fl oz/30 ml) of milk, again beating until well mixed. To the third portion, add the orange zest (rind) and orange juice.

Preheat the oven to 375°F (190°C/Gas 5).

Spoon small amounts of the dough into the mold, alternating the 3 portions, until all of the dough is used. Cover with a damp cloth and let stand in a warm place for about 30 minutes, or until the dough has doubled in bulk and almost fills the mold.

Bake for 60–80 minutes, or until a skewer inserted in the middle of the cake comes out clean. Stand for 10 minutes in the mold, then turn out onto a wire rack to cool completely.

Dust with sugar and serve immediately.

COCONUT CAKE

Serves 10–12

1/2 cup (4 oz/125 g) butter
1 cup (8 oz/250 g) sugar
2 eggs
2/3 cup (1 oz/30 g)
flaked (desiccated) coconut
1 1/2 cups (6 oz/185 g)
self-rising flour, sifted
1 cup (8 fl oz/250 ml) sour cream
1/3 cup (3 fl oz/90 ml) cream

ICING

2 cups (3 1/2 oz/100 g) shredded coconut
2 egg whites
1/2 cup (3 oz/90 g)
confectioners' (icing) sugar, sifted
1 drop red food coloring (optional)

Preheat the oven to 350°F (180°C/Gas 4). Butter a 9-inch (23-cm) round springform pan and line the base with parchment or waxed (greaseproof) paper. Cream the butter and sugar in a bowl until light and fluffy.

Add the eggs, one at a time, beating well after each addition. Stir in a little of the coconut, flour, sour cream, and cream, then stir in a little more of each ingredient. Repeat until all ingredients are used and the mixture is smooth.

Pour the mixture into the prepared pan. Bake for 1 hour, or until a skewer inserted in the middle of the cake comes out clean. Let the cake rest in the pan for 5 minutes before turning out onto a wire rack to cool completely.

Icing: Combine the coconut and egg whites in a bowl, mixing well. Add the sugar in batches, stirring well after each addition. If desired, red food coloring may be added to the icing. Cover the top of the cake with the icing and serve.

COCONUT CAKE

1. Cream the butter and sugar until light and fluffy.

2. Add the eggs, one at a time, beating well after each addition.

3. Stir in alternately the coconut, sifted flour, sour cream, and cream.

4. Stir until smooth.

ABOVE AND OPPOSITE: Coconut Cake

ORANGE LAYER CAKE
Serves 10–12

3 eggs
1 cup (8 oz/250 g) sugar
1 teaspoon orange juice
1 teaspoon grated orange zest (rind)
1³/₄ cups (7 oz/220 g) all-purpose
(plain) flour
¹/₄ cup (1¹/₂ oz/45 g)
cornstarch (cornflour)
1¹/₂ teaspoons baking powder
1 teaspoon baking soda (bicarbonate of soda)
1 cup (8 fl oz/250 ml) sour cream
1 cup (8 oz/250 g)
sweet (unsalted) butter, melted

ICING
1 cup (8 oz/250 g) sweet (unsalted) butter
2 tablespoons orange juice
2¹/₂ cups (13 oz/410 g) confectioners'
(icing) sugar, sifted
¹/₄ cup (2 fl oz/65 ml) Cointreau or
Grand Marnier

Preheat the oven to 350°F (180°C/Gas 4). Butter and flour two 9-inch (23-cm) round cake pans. In a large bowl, combine the eggs with the sugar, orange juice, and orange zest (rind) and beat until creamy, about 3–4 minutes. Sift together the flour, cornstarch (cornflour), baking powder, and baking soda (bicarbonate of soda). In a separate bowl, combine the sour cream and melted butter. Fold the flour and sour cream mixtures alternately into the creamed mixture.
Pour the mixture evenly into the prepared pans. Bake for 20–25 minutes, or until a skewer inserted in the middle of each cake comes out clean. Cool the cake layers in the pan for 10 minutes before turning out onto a wire rack to cool completely.
Icing: Beat the butter until it is light and fluffy. Stir in the orange juice, and then gradually beat in the sugar until smooth.

OPPOSITE: Orange Layer Cake

When each cake is cool, cut in half horizontally. Place the bottom layer on a serving platter and brush with the Cointreau or Grand Marnier. Spread with 3–4 tablespoons of icing. Repeat with the remaining layers. To finish, cover the cake with the remaining icing. Cut the cake into wedges and serve.

•

GINGER BROWNIES
Serves 6–8

3 tablespoons (1¹/₂ oz/45 g) sweet
(unsalted) butter
4 oz (125 g) semisweet
(dark) chocolate, chopped
2 eggs
³/₄ cup (6 oz/185 g) sugar
1 teaspoon vanilla extract (essence)
¹/₂ cup (2 oz/60 g)
all-purpose (plain) flour, sifted
¹/₂ teaspoon baking powder
¹/₂ cup (2 oz/60 g)
finely chopped walnuts
¹/₃ cup (2¹/₂ oz/75 g)
chopped dried or glacéed figs
3 tablespoons (1¹/₂ oz/45 g) glacéed ginger
12 chocolate fudge cookies, broken into pieces

Preheat the oven to 350°F (180°C/Gas 4). Butter an 8-inch (20-cm) square cake pan.
Heat the butter over a low heat and when half melted stir in the chocolate until melted and combined. Remove from the heat and set aside. Beat the eggs until light and fluffy. Gradually add the sugar and beat until the mixture is pale and thick, about 3–4 minutes. Combine the melted chocolate and butter with the remaining ingredients and fold into the egg mixture. Pour the mixture into the prepared pan. Bake for 40 minutes, or until the center of the cake feels firm to the touch. Cool completely in the pan before turning out. Cut the brownies into squares and serve.

CINNAMON & DATE RING
Serves 8

CAKE
2 cups (8 oz/250 g) self-rising flour
Pinch of salt
1/4 cup (2 oz/60 g) butter
1/4 cup (1 1/2 oz/45 g)
confectioners' (icing) sugar
1 egg yolk
3/4 cup (6 fl oz/185 ml) milk
1/2 cup (2 1/2 oz/75 g)
finely chopped fresh dates
1/3 cup (2 oz/60 g) packed brown sugar
1/4 cup (1 oz/30 g) chopped walnuts
1 teaspoon ground cinnamon
2 tablespoons (1 oz/30 g) butter, melted

GLAZE
1 egg white, lightly beaten
Confectioners' (icing) sugar, for dusting

Preheat the oven to 425°F (220°C/Gas 7). Butter a baking sheet.

Cake: Sift the flour and salt into a bowl. Rub in the butter until the mixture resembles coarse breadcrumbs, then stir in the sugar. Mix the egg yolk and milk together, then add to the sugar mixture, stirring in quickly with a knife. Turn out onto a floured board and pat into a 12 x 6-inch (30 x 15-cm) rectangle.

Mix together the dates, brown sugar, walnuts, cinnamon, and butter and spread over the dough, then roll up to make a 12-inch (30-cm) long roll.

Glaze: Form the dough into a ring, joining the ends with a little of the beaten egg white. Cut large slits in the ring and brush the top with the rest of the egg white.

Place on the prepared baking sheet and bake for 20–25 minutes, or until puffed and golden.

Serve warm, dusted with sugar.

PREVIOUS PAGES: Cinnamon & Date Ring (top) and Ginger Brownies (bottom)
OPPOSITE: Cherry Cake with Almond Streusel

CHERRY CAKE WITH ALMOND STREUSEL
Serves 10–12

3/4 cup plus 1 tablespoon
(6 1/2 oz/200 g) butter
1 cup (8 oz/250 g) sugar
2 eggs
2 1/4 cups (9 oz/280 g)
all-purpose (plain) flour, sifted
2 teaspoons baking powder
1 cup (8 oz/250 g) bottled or canned
red cherries, pitted and drained
1 teaspoon ground allspice

STREUSEL TOPPING
1/4 cup (2 oz/60 g) butter, chopped
1/2 cup (2 oz/60 g) all-purpose (plain) flour
1/4 cup (2 oz/60 g) superfine (caster) sugar
1/3 cup (1 1/2 oz/45 g) sliced (flaked) almonds
1/2 teaspoon ground allspice
Heavy (double) cream or ice cream, for serving

Preheat the oven to 350°F (180°C/Gas 4). Lightly grease an 8-inch (20-cm) springform pan and line the base with parchment or waxed (greaseproof) paper.

Cream the butter and sugar in a bowl until light and fluffy. Add the eggs, one at a time, beating well. Fold in the flour and baking powder and mix well.

Spread half of the cake batter evenly onto the base of the prepared pan. Top with the cherries, then sprinkle with the allspice. Spread the remaining cake batter over the cherries.

Streusel Topping: Rub the butter into the flour until the mixture resembles breadcrumbs. Mix in the sugar and almonds until well combined.

Press the streusel topping on top of the cake. Sprinkle with the allspice. Bake for 45 minutes, or until a skewer inserted in the middle of the cake comes out clean. Let the cake rest in the pan for 10 minutes before turning out onto a wire rack to cool completely.

Serve warm or cold with cream or ice cream.

PECAN COFFEE CAKE

Serves 10–12

³/₄ cup (6 oz/185 g) butter, softened
1¹/₂ cups (12 oz/375 g) sugar
3 eggs
2 teaspoons vanilla extract (essence)
3 cups (12 oz/375 g) all-purpose (plain) flour
1¹/₂ teaspoons baking powder
1¹/₂ teaspoons baking soda
(bicarbonate of soda)
¹/₂ teaspoon salt
2 cups (16 fl oz/500 ml) sour cream

FILLING
³/₄ cup (4 oz/125 g) packed brown sugar
1 tablespoon ground cinnamon
1¹/₂ tablespoons unsweetened cocoa powder
³/₄ cup (4 oz/125 g) raisins
³/₄ cup (3 oz/90 g) chopped pecans

ICING
²/₃ cup (5 fl oz/155 ml) cream
1 tablespoon strong black coffee
1–2 tablespoons confectioners' (icing)
sugar, sifted

Preheat the oven to 350°F (180°C/Gas 4). Butter a 9-inch (23-cm) springform pan and line the base with parchment or waxed (greaseproof) paper.

Cake: Cream the butter and sugar until light and fluffy. Beat in the eggs, one at a time, beating well after each addition. Beat in the vanilla. Sift together the flour, baking powder, baking soda (bicarbonate of soda), and salt. Fold in the sifted dry ingredients alternating with the sour cream, beginning and ending with the flour mixture.

Spread a third of the batter into the prepared pan.

Filling: Combine the sugar, cinnamon, cocoa, raisins, and pecans and mix well.

Sprinkle half of the pecan filling evenly over the first layer of batter. Continue layering the remaining batter and filling in the same manner, finishing with a layer of the batter. Rap the pan on a hard surface several times to expel any bubbles.

Bake for 50–60 minutes, or until a skewer inserted in the middle of the cake comes out clean. Allow the cake to cool in the pan for 10 minutes before turning out onto a wire rack to cool completely.

Icing: Whip the cream until soft peaks form. Fold in the coffee and then the sugar and mix well. When the cake is cool, spread the icing over the top and serve.

PECAN COFFEE CAKE

1. Combine the sugar, cinnamon, cocoa powder, raisins, and pecans.

3. Spread a third of the batter into the pan and sprinkle it evenly with half of the pecan filling.

2. Cream the butter and sugar, beat in the eggs. Fold in the combined sifted flour, baking powder, and baking soda alternately with the sour cream.

4. Continue to layer the remaining batter and filling, ending with a layer of the batter.

OPPOSITE: Pecan Coffee Cake

GERMAN BUTTER CAKE
Serves 10-12

1 tablespoon active dry yeast
$^1/_2$ cup (4 oz/125 g) sugar
$^1/_2$ cup (4 fl oz/125 ml) lukewarm water
1 teaspoon salt
$^1/_2$ cup (4 oz/125 g) sweet (unsalted) butter
$^3/_4$ cup (6 fl oz/185 ml) milk
1 vanilla bean, split
Grated zest (rind) of 1 lemon
3 large eggs
4 cups (1 lb/500 g) all-purpose (plain) flour

TOPPING
$^3/_4$ cup (6 oz/185 g) sweet (unsalted)
butter, softened
$^1/_2$ cup (4 oz/125 g) sugar
$^3/_4$ cup (4 oz/125 g) packed brown sugar
$^1/_3$ cup ($1^1/_2$ oz/45 g) ground almonds
$^1/_3$ cup ($1^1/_2$ oz/45 g) ground walnuts
$^1/_2$ teaspoon ground cinnamon
$^1/_2$ teaspoon vanilla extract (essence)

Butter a 13 x 9 x 2-inch (33 x 23 x 5-cm) baking pan. In a small bowl, combine the yeast, 1 tablespoon of the sugar, and the warm water and set aside in a warm place for 15 minutes, or until bubbles appear. In another bowl combine the remaining scant $^1/_2$ cup ($3^1/_2$ oz/100g) sugar, and the salt, and butter. Pour the milk into a saucepan, add the vanilla bean and bring to a boil. Remove from the heat, scrape out the seeds, discard the vanilla bean, and stir the milk into the butter mixture. Let the mixture stand until it is lukewarm. Stir in the yeast mixture and lemon zest (rind). Add the eggs, one at a time, beating well after each addition. Fold in the flour, a little at a time. Beat the dough for 5 minutes, or until smooth.

Spread the dough into the prepared pan. Cover loosely with a tea towel and set aside in a warm place for 30–45 minutes to allow the mixture to rise, almost doubling in size.

Preheat the oven to 400°F (200°C/Gas 6).

Topping: Cream the butter, sugar, and brown sugar until light and fluffy. Stir in the almonds, walnuts, cinnamon, and vanilla. Drop teaspoonfuls of the topping onto the dough.

Bake the cake for 35 minutes, or until the top is golden and a skewer inserted in the middle comes out clean. Allow the cake to cool completely in the pan.

Cut into wedges and serve with butter.

BELOW AND OPPOSITE: German Butter Cake

Mini Cakes

•

Good things do, indeed, come in small packages, and these great-tasting single serves are evidence. If you live alone, want to add a sweet surprise to the lunch box, or provide a delicious party souvenir, a cupcake, muffin, or madeleine from this selection is bound to fit the bill.

MADELEINES
Makes 24

4 eggs
³/₄ cup (6 oz/185 g) sugar
1 cup (4 oz/125 g) all-purpose
(plain) flour, sifted
1 teaspoon baking powder
¹/₂ cup (4 oz/125 g) sweet (unsalted)
butter, melted and cooled
Confectioners' (icing) sugar, for dusting

Preheat the oven to 425°F (220°C/Gas 7). Brush the indentations of a madeleine pan with a little melted butter.

Combine the eggs and sugar and beat until pale and thick. Fold in the flour and baking powder in 3 batches, adding the butter with the last batch. Cover and refrigerate for 10 minutes.

Spoon 1–2 tablespoons of the batter into each mold and bake for 5 minutes. Reduce the heat to 400°F (200°C/Gas 6) and bake for another 5 minutes, or until each cake has a small peak in the center and feels spongy to the touch. Transfer to a wire rack to cool.

Serve dusted with confectioners' (icing) sugar.

PREVIOUS PAGES: Madeleines
BELOW AND OPPOSITE :
Fruit & Chocolate Chip Cupcakes

FRUIT & CHOCOLATE CHIP CUPCAKES
Makes about 24

4 eggs
²/₃ cup (5 oz/155 g) sugar
1¹/₄ cups (5 oz/155 g)
all-purpose (plain) flour
1 teaspoon baking powder
²/₃ cup (5 oz/155 g) butter, melted
¹/₃ cup (1¹/₂ oz/45 g) chopped dried apricots
1 tablespoon chopped glacéed green cherries
2 tablespoons chopped glacéed red cherries
1 tablespoon currants
1 tablespoon chopped blanched almonds
¹/₂ cup (2¹/₂ oz/75 g) chocolate chips
1 tablespoon chopped glacéed ginger

Preheat the oven to 400°F (200°C/Gas 6). Lightly grease two mini (1¹/₂–2-tablespoon capacity) muffin pans.

Beat the eggs and sugar until thick and pale, about 5 minutes. Fold in all of the remaining ingredients. Cover, then refrigerate for 25 minutes.

Place 1 tablespoon of the mixture into each muffin mold. Bake for 15 minutes, or until cooked through and a skewer inserted in the middle of one of the cakes comes out clean. Cool in the pan for 2–3 minutes before turning out onto a wire rack to cool completely.

Serve warm or cool.

KINGS' & QUEENS' CONVERSATIONS
Makes 6–8

DOUGH
2 cups (8 oz/250 g) all-purpose (plain) flour
$^1/_4$ cup (2 oz/60 g) sugar
$^1/_3$ cup plus 2 teaspoons ($3^1/_2$ oz/100 g)
sweet (unsalted) butter, chopped
3 egg yolks
$^1/_2$ teaspoon vanilla extract (essence)

ALMOND FILLING
$^1/_4$ cup ($1^1/_2$ oz/45 g) confectioners'
(icing) sugar
1 cup ($3^1/_2$ oz/100 g) ground almonds
$^1/_4$ cup plus 1 tablespoon ($2^1/_2$ oz/75 g)
sweet (unsalted) butter, softened
2 large eggs
1 tablespoon rum
1 egg yolk, beaten
Confectioners' (icing) sugar, for dusting

Dough: In a large bowl combine the flour and sugar. Rub in the butter until the mixture resembles breadcrumbs. Add the egg yolks and vanilla and, working quickly, form a smooth dough. Roll into a ball, wrap in plastic wrap and refrigerate for 30 minutes.

Preheat the oven to 400°F (200°C/Gas 6). Butter a mini ($1^1/_2$–2 tablespoon-capacity) muffin pan.

Almond Filling: In a bowl combine all the ingredients, apart from the confectioners' sugar, and beat until smooth.

Reserving one-third of the dough for decoration, press the remainder into the prepared muffin molds and fill with 1 tablespoon of the almond filling, so that the mold is three-fourths full. Roll the reserved dough into thin coils and use to decorate the top of each tart. Brush each tart with a little beaten egg yolk and bake for 25–30 minutes, or until golden.

Serve dusted with confectioners' sugar, if desired.

Kings' & Queens' Conversations

COCONUT & RASPBERRY CUPCAKES
Makes 32

4 eggs
²/₃ cup (5 oz/155 g) sugar
1¹/₄ cups (5 oz/155 g)
all-purpose (plain) flour
1 teaspoon baking powder
²/₃ cup (2 oz/60 g) flaked (desiccated) coconut
¹/₂ cup (4 oz/125 g)
sweet (unsalted) butter, melted
¹/₄ cup (3 oz/90 g) raspberry preserves
Confectioners' (icing) sugar, for dusting

Preheat the oven to 425°F (220°C/Gas 7). Butter 3 cupcake or mini (1¹/₂–2-tablespoon capacity) muffin pans or fit with paper liners. If you do not have enough pans, the cakes may be cooked in batches instead.

In a large bowl, whisk the eggs and sugar together until the mixture is thick and pale and forms a ribbon. Sift the flour and baking powder together and fold into the egg mixture alternately with the coconut. Fold in the melted butter, then chill in the refrigerator for 25 minutes.

Place 2 teaspoons of the batter into the prepared molds, dot ¹/₂ teaspoon of preserves in the center of each, then top with another 2 teaspoons of batter so that each muffin cup is three-fourths full. Bake for 5 minutes, reduce the heat to 400°F (200°C/Gas 6) and bake for a further 5–7 minutes, or until risen and golden. Turn out onto wire racks to cool completely.

Dust with the sugar and serve.

COCONUT & RASPBERRY CUPCAKES

1. Combine the eggs and sugar in a large bowl. Whisk until the mixture is thick and pale and forms a ribbon.

3. Fold in the melted butter.

2. Sift the combined flour and baking powder and fold into the egg mixture alternately with the coconut.

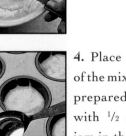

4. Place 2 teaspoons of the mixture into the prepared pans. Dot with ¹/₂ teaspoon of jam in the center and top with another 2 teaspoons of batter.

ABOVE AND OPPOSITE: Coconut & Raspberry Cupcakes

BABA CAKES
Makes 10

1 envelope (¹/₄ oz/7 g) dried yeast
¹/₂ cup (4 fl oz/125 ml) warm water
1³/₄ cups (7 oz/220 g)
all-purpose (plain) flour
4 eggs
¹/₄ cup (2 oz/60 g) sugar
Pinch salt
¹/₂ cup (4 oz/125 g) sweet (unsalted)
butter, softened and chopped

GLAZE
1 cup (8 oz/250 g) sugar
1 cup (8 fl oz/250 ml) water
¹/₂ cup (4 fl oz/125 ml) rum
Heavy (double) cream, for serving
Seasonal berries, for serving (optional)

Stir the yeast into the water and let stand for 5 minutes to dissolve. Add ¹/₂ cup (2 oz/60 g) of the flour and, using an electric beater, mix until combined and the mixture is smooth, about 1–2 minutes. Beat in the eggs, one at a time, beating well after each addition. Add the sugar and salt and the remaining 1¹/₄ cups (5 oz/155 g) flour, beating until the mixture is smooth. Cover and let stand in a warm place until doubled in bulk, about 45 minutes.

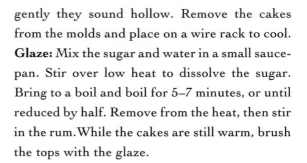

Gradually beat in the softened butter, piece by piece until the mixture is smooth. Set aside.
Butter ten ³/₄-cup Baba molds. Place 2–3 tablespoons of the mixture in each mold, cover and let stand for 45 minutes, or until doubled in bulk.
Meanwhile, preheat the oven to 400°F (200°C/Gas 6). Add the cakes and bake for 20 minutes, or until puffed and golden and when tapped

ABOVE AND OPPOSITE: Baba Cakes

gently they sound hollow. Remove the cakes from the molds and place on a wire rack to cool.
Glaze: Mix the sugar and water in a small saucepan. Stir over low heat to dissolve the sugar. Bring to a boil and boil for 5–7 minutes, or until reduced by half. Remove from the heat, then stir in the rum. While the cakes are still warm, brush the tops with the glaze.
Serve warm or cool with the cream and seasonal berries, if desired.

•

CHOCOLATE CHERRY MUFFINS
Makes 6 large muffins

2 cups (8 oz/250 g) self-rising flour
1 teaspoon ground allspice
¹/₄ cup (1 oz/30 g) ground almonds
¹/₃ cup (2 oz/60 g) packed brown sugar
1 egg
¹/₃ cup (3 oz/90 g) butter, melted
²/₃ cup (5¹/₂ fl oz/170 ml) buttermilk
1 cup (5 oz/155 g) chocolate chips
1 cup (6 oz/185 g) bottled or canned red cherries, pitted and drained

Preheat the oven to 350°F (180°C/Gas 4). Grease a 6-cup large muffin pan. Sift the flour and allspice into a large bowl. Stir in the almonds, sugar, egg, butter, buttermilk, chocolate, and cherries. Mix lightly with a fork until just combined.
Spoon the mixture evenly into the prepared muffin pan. Bake for 20–25 minutes, or until a skewer inserted in the middle of one of the muffins comes out clean. Cool in the pan for 10 minutes before turning out onto a wire rack to cool further.
Serve warm or cool.

STRAWBERRY SHORTCAKES

Makes 8

CAKE

2 cups (8 oz/250 g)
all-purpose (plain) flour
2 tablespoons sugar
2 teaspoons baking powder
$^1/_2$ teaspoon salt
2 tablespoons sweet (unsalted)
butter, cut into pieces
$1^1/_2$ teaspoons grated lemon zest (rind)
$^3/_4$ cup (6 fl oz/185 ml)
heavy (double) cream
$^1/_4$ cup (2 fl oz/60 ml) milk
2 tablespoons
sweet (unsalted) butter, softened

FILLING

8 oz (250 g) strawberries, hulled
and chopped
$^1/_4$ cup (2 oz/60 g) sugar
1 teaspoon lemon juice
1 cup (8 fl oz/250 ml)
heavy (double) cream, whipped
Extra strawberries, to decorate

Preheat the oven to 400°F (200°C/Gas 6). Butter a baking sheet.

Cake: Sift together the flour, sugar, baking powder, and salt. Blend in the butter and lemon zest (rind), and mix until the mixture resembles bread crumbs. Stir in enough cream, a little at a time, to make a soft dough. On a floured surface, form the dough into a ball and roll or pat it out to $^1/_2$ inch (1 cm) thick. Cut into rounds with a 3-inch ($7^1/_2$-cm) cutter dipped in flour, then arrange the rounds on the prepared baking sheet. Form the scraps gently into a ball, and repeat. Brush the tops of the rounds lightly with milk. Bake in

PREVIOUS PAGES: Chocolate Cherry Muffins (left) and Strawberry Shortcakes (right)
OPPOSITE: Chocolate Truffle Cupcakes

the middle of the oven for 15–20 minutes, or until puffed and golden. Split the cakes horizontally with a fork and while still warm spread the halves with the softened butter.

Filling: Combine the strawberries, sugar and lemon juice in a small saucepan. Bring to a boil and cook over a moderate heat, stirring constantly for 5 minutes. Transfer the mixture to a bowl and cool completely.

Cover the bottom halves of the cakes with the strawberry mixture and some of the cream. Top with the cake tops and cream, and decorate with strawberries. Serve immediately.

•

CHOCOLATE TRUFFLE CUPCAKES

Makes about 12

$^1/_2$ cup (4 oz/125 g) butter
$^3/_4$ cup (6 oz/185 g) sugar
2 eggs
$6^1/_2$ oz (200 g) bittersweet (dark)
chocolate, melted
2 cups (8 oz/250 g) self-rising flour
2 tablespoons unsweetened cocoa powder
1 teaspoon baking powder
1 cup (8 fl oz/250 ml) milk
12 Hershey's kisses or chocolate buttons,
for decoration

Preheat the oven to 400°F (200°C/Gas 6). Lightly grease a 12-cup capacity muffin pan.

Cream the butter and sugar until light and fluffy. Add the eggs, one at a time, beating well after each addition. Stir in the chocolate, flour, cocoa powder, and baking powder alternately with the milk. Spoon the mixture into the prepared pans and top each cake with a chocolate button. Bake for 20 minutes, or until cooked and a skewer inserted in the middle of one of the cakes comes out clean. Turn the cupcakes out onto a wire rack to cool completely. Serve warm or cool with freshly brewed coffee.

Indulgences

·

Over-the-top, hang-the-calories creations that
are designed to raise the spirits and taste as good
as they look. Spoil yourself or someone special
with these tastes of the high life.

ALMOND & APRICOT TRUFFLE CAKE
Serves 10–12

2¹/₄ cups (9 oz/280 g) self-rising flour
¹/₂ cup (2 oz/60 g) all-purpose
(plain) flour
1¹/₂ cups (5¹/₂ oz/170 g) ground
almonds
1 cup (8 oz/250 g) butter
1 cup (8 oz/250 g) sugar
1 cup (8 fl oz/250 ml) apricot
or peach nectar
6 eggs

CHOCOLATE BUTTERCREAM
1 cup (8 oz/250 g) butter
8 oz (250 g) semisweet
(dark) chocolate, chopped

WHITE CHOCOLATE TRUFFLES
¹/₄ cup (2 oz/60 g) butter
6¹/₂ oz (200 g) white chocolate,
coarsely chopped
¹/₂ cup (4 oz/125 g) confectioners'
(icing) sugar, sifted

DARK CHOCOLATE TRUFFLES
¹/₄ cup (2 oz/60 g) butter
6¹/₂ oz (200 g) semisweet
(dark) chocolate
¹/₄ cup (2 fl oz/60 ml) cream
¹/₂ cup (3 oz/90 g) unsweetened cocoa
powder, sifted

SPUN SUGAR
2¹/₂ cups (1 lb/500g)
superfine (caster) sugar
³/₄ cup (6 fl oz/185 ml) water

Preheat the oven to 350°F (180°C/Gas 4). Butter two 9-inch (23-cm) round cake pans and line with parchment or waxed (greaseproof) paper. Sift the flours into a bowl, add the almonds and mix well, making a well in the center.

Combine the butter, sugar, and apricot nectar in a saucepan. Stir over a low heat until the butter and sugar are melted; cool slightly. Pour into the flour mixture, mixing until smooth. Add the eggs, one at a time, mixing well after each addition. Divide the mixture evenly between the prepared pans. Bake in the oven for 35 minutes, or until a skewer inserted in the middle of each cake comes out clean. Let stand for 5 minutes before turning out onto a wire rack to cool completely.

Chocolate Buttercream: Melt the butter and chocolate in the top of a double boiler over a low heat until melted and smooth. Cool until the mixture is spreadable.

Cut each cake in half horizontally and place 3 tablespoons of the chocolate buttercream between the layers. Spread the sides and top of the cake with the remaining chocolate buttercream.

White Chocolate Truffles: In a saucepan, melt the butter, then add the chocolate. Remove from the heat and stir until smooth. Chill in the refrigerator, about 5 minutes, until slightly firm. Roll the mixture into teaspoon-sized balls and coat in the sugar. Freeze or refrigerate the truffles until firm, 10–15 minutes.

Dark Chocolate Truffles: In a saucepan, melt the butter, then add the chocolate. Remove from the heat and stir until smooth. Mix in the cream, stirring well. Roll the mixture into balls, then coat in the cocoa. Freeze or refrigerate the truffles until firm, 10–15 minutes.

Spun Sugar: Place a 3¹/₄ ft (1-m) long strip of parchment or waxed (greaseproof) paper over a work bench.

In a heavy-based saucepan, combine the sugar and water and stir over medium heat until the sugar is dissolved, about 2 minutes. Bring to a boil and cook, without stirring, until golden in color, 10–15 minutes. Remove from the heat. Dip 2 forks in the saucepan and form long strands by flicking the toffee from one end of the paper to the other. Working quickly, mold the strands into a crown.

Decorate the top of the cake with the truffles and spun sugar and serve immediately.

RICH ALMOND CAKE
Serves 8–10

9 eggs, separated
¹/₄ cup (2 fl oz/60 ml) brandy,
amaretto or rum
1 teaspoon vanilla extract (essence)
1 cup (8 oz/250 g) sugar
2¹/₄ cups (8 oz/250 g) ground almonds
³/₄ cup (3 oz/90 g) dry breadcrumbs
2 teaspoons baking powder
¹/₂ cup (4 oz/125 g) sugar

SYRUP
2 tablespoons brandy, amaretto, or rum
1 tablespoon sugar

FILLING AND TOPPING
1¹/₄ cups (10 fl oz/315 ml)
heavy (double) cream, whipped
1¹/₃ cups (5 oz/155 g) flaked almonds, toasted

Preheat the oven to 300°F (150°C/Gas 2). Butter two 8-inch (20 cm) round cake pans and line with parchment or waxed (greaseproof) paper. Combine the egg yolks, brandy, vanilla, and sugar in a large mixing bowl and beat until pale and thick, 3–4 minutes. Stir in the ground almonds, breadcrumbs, and baking powder. In a separate bowl, beat the egg whites until stiff. Gradually add the sugar and beat until dissolved, about 1 minute. Fold one-third of the egg whites into the egg yolk mixture, then fold in the remaining egg whites.

Pour the mixture into the prepared pans. Bake for 45 minutes, or until a skewer inserted in the center of the cake comes out clean. Cool in the pans for 2–3 minutes before turning out onto a wire rack to cool completely.

Syrup: Combine the brandy and sugar in a small saucepan and stir over low heat to dissolve the sugar.

Make holes in the top of each cake layer using a skewer and brush with the syrup.

Filling and Topping: Place the bottom cake layer on a serving plate and spread with half of the cream. Set the other layer on top and cover with the remaining cream. Press the almonds onto the cake and serve immediately.

PREVIOUS PAGES: Almond & Apricot Truffle Cake
ABOVE: Rich Almond Cake

HUMMINGBIRD CAKE
Serves 10–12

6 medium, ripe bananas
$^3/_4$ cup (6 fl oz/185 ml) grapeseed oil
4 eggs
$6^1/_2$ oz (200 g) canned pineapple slices
1 cup (8 fl oz/250 ml) pineapple juice
1 teaspoon vanilla extract (essence)
4 cups (1 lb/500 g) all-purpose (plain) flour
1 cup (8 oz/250 g) sugar
4 teaspoons baking powder
$^1/_2$ teaspoon salt
1 tablespoon ground cardamom
or garam masala

ICING AND FILLING
$^1/_2$ cup (4 oz/125 g) sweet (unsalted) butter
2 tablespoons sour cream
$2^1/_2$ cups (1 lb/500 g)
confectioners' (icing) sugar
8 oz (250 g) cream cheese
1 large ripe mango or 12 oz (375 g)
canned mango, sliced finely
Fresh edible flower petals, for decoration

Preheat the oven to 350°F (180°C/Gas 4). Butter three 9-inch (23-cm) springform cake pans and line with baking parchment or waxed (greaseproof) paper.

Combine the bananas, oil, eggs, pineapple slices, and pineapple juice in the bowl of a food processor and process until combined. Transfer to a large bowl and fold in the remaining ingredients. Pour into the prepared pans, dividing the batter evenly. Bake for 30–35 minutes, or until the cakes come away from the sides of the pan. Let the cakes cool in the pans for 10 minutes before turning out onto a wire rack to cool completely.

Icing and Filling: Process the butter, sour cream, sugar, and cream cheese until smooth and combined, about 1 minute. Do not overprocess as it will become runny.

To assemble the cake, place the bottom layer on a serving plate and cover with one-third of the icing. Spread with half of the mango slices. Top with the second cake layer and repeat, using another third of the icing and all of the remaining mango slices. Place the third cake layer on top and cover with the last of the icing. Decorate with the fresh flowers, if desired, and serve.

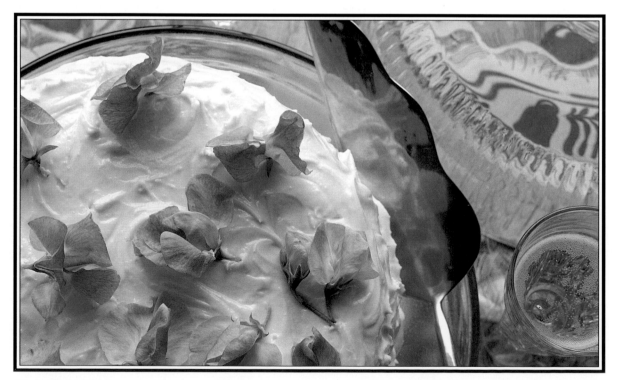

Hummingbird Cake

GATEAU SAINT HONORÉ
Serves 10–12

½ cup (4 oz/125 g) butter
½ cup (4 oz/125 g) sugar
1 egg yolk
1 cup (4 oz/125 g) all-purpose
(plain) flour
1 teaspoon vanilla extract (essence)
Water or orange juice, as required
½ cup (4 oz/125 g) butter
1 cup (8 fl oz/250 ml) water
1 cup (4 oz/125 g) all-purpose
(plain) flour
4 large eggs

CUSTARD FILLING
1 cup (8 fl oz/250 ml) milk
½ cup (4 oz/125 g) sugar
1 vanilla bean, split
¼ cup (1 oz/30 g) cornstarch (cornflour)
2 eggs, plus 3 egg yolks
8 strawberries, to decorate

TOFFEE
1 cup (8 oz/250 g) sugar
½ cup (4 fl oz/125 ml) water
2 teaspoons white vinegar

Preheat the oven to 350°F (180°C/Gas 4).
Cream the butter, sugar, and egg yolk in a food processor until light and fluffy. Add the flour and vanilla and process to form a manageable dough, adding a little water or orange juice if required. Lightly knead the dough into a ball, cover with plastic wrap, and refrigerate for 30 minutes.

Roll out pastry to form a 9–10-inch (23–25-cm) circle and place on a nonstick baking sheet. Bake for 15–20 minutes, or until golden. Transfer to a wire rack and cool.

Increase the oven temperature to 400°F (200°C/Gas 6). Heat the butter and water in a small saucepan until small bubbles begin to appear in the base of the saucepan. Add the flour all at once and cook over a low heat for 2 minutes, stirring constantly, being careful to ensure the mixture doesn't burn.

Transfer the mixture to a bowl. Using an electric mixer, beat, adding the eggs one at a time, until the mixture is smooth and glossy.

Butter a baking sheet thoroughly and shake a little water over the top.

Using a pastry (piping) bag fitted with a large plain nozzle, pipe a ring of choux pastry 1 inch (2.5 cm) smaller than the pastry base. Pipe the remaining choux pastry into 8 ball-shaped puffs. Bake for 20 minutes, or until the pastry is risen and golden. Remove from the baking sheet, place on a wire rack and let cool. Cut the pastry puffs open and remove any uncooked pastry from inside.

Custard Filling: In a large saucepan, bring the milk, sugar, and vanilla bean to a boil. Remove from the heat and remove the vanilla bean. Whisk the cornstarch (cornflour), eggs, and egg yolks together in a bowl. Gradually whisk in the heated milk mixture and then return the custard to the saucepan. Gently heat until the custard is slightly thickened and coats the back of a wooden spoon, about 5 minutes. Cover the surface of the custard with plastic wrap and refrigerate until firm, about 15 minutes. Place the pastry circle on a serving plate. Place the choux pastry ring on the circle, then spoon the custard into the center. Arrange the choux puffs on top. Decorate with the strawberries.

Toffee: Combine all of the ingredients in a heavy-based saucepan and stir over low heat until the sugar dissolves, about 2 minutes. Brush the side of the pan with water to wash any sugar crystals away. Bring the toffee to a boil and cook without stirring until it is a golden color, about 5 minutes. Reserving a small amount of toffee, pour the remainder over the cake and strawberries. With a wooden spoon, draw out thin strands of the remaining toffee and spin these strands around the handle of the spoon. When a large amount of toffee has been spun, remove it from the wooden spoon. Decorate the top of the cake with the spun toffee and serve.

LE CONCORDE
Serves 10–12

3 eggs, separated
³/₄ cup (6 oz/185 g) sugar
1 cup (4 oz/125 g) self-rising flour
1 teaspoon melted butter
1 teaspoon vanilla extract (essence)
2 tablespoons hot water

CHOCOLATE GANACHE
1¹/₄ cups (10 fl oz/315 ml) cream
1 lb (500 g) semisweet (dark) chocolate

CHOCOLATE SQUARES
8 oz (250 g) semisweet (dark)
chocolate, melted
8 oz (250 g) white chocolate, melted

DECORATION
4 oz (125 g) white chocolate, melted
Unsweetened cocoa powder, for dusting

Preheat the oven to 350°F (180°C/Gas 4). Grease two 9-inch (23-cm) round cake pans.
Beat the egg whites until stiff. Gradually add the sugar, then fold in the egg yolks, flour, butter, vanilla, and water. Pour the mixture into the prepared pans. Bake for 20 minutes, or until a skewer inserted in the middle of each cake comes out clean. Cool in the pans for 5 minutes before turning out onto wire racks to cool completely.
Chocolate Ganache: Heat the cream and chocolate together until the chocolate melts. Refrigerate until firm enough to handle, about 15 minutes. Use to sandwich the cakes together and to coat the outside of the cake. Any excess ganache can be piped onto the cake for decoration.
Chocolate Squares: Spread the semisweet (dark) chocolate onto a nonstick baking sheet. Cool slightly in the refrigerator until firm enough to

RIGHT: Double Chocolate No-bake Cheesecake
PREVIOUS PAGES: Gateau Saint Honoré (left) and Le Concorde (right)

handle, about 15 minutes, then use a cake comb to make patterns in the chocolate. Allow the chocolate to set firmly, refrigerating for 5–8 minutes. Spread the white chocolate over the dark chocolate and allow this to set, refrigerating for about 10 minutes. Cut the chocolate into squares and lift off the baking sheet. Arrange the chocolate squares around the cake.
Decoration: Spread the melted chocolate onto a marble board until ¹/₈ inch (5 mm) thick. Allow the chocolate to set in the refrigerator, about 10 minutes. Using a sharp knife at a 45° angle, run the knife over the chocolate so that it scrapes up the chocolate to form curls. (The more pressure placed on the knife, the thicker the curls will be.) Use these curls to decorate the center of the cake. Refrigerate the cake until required. Sift the cocoa and use to dust the cake just before serving.

•

DOUBLE CHOCOLATE NO-BAKE CHEESECAKE
Serves 8–10

BASE
4 oz (125 g) chocolate cookies (biscuits)
¹/₄ cup (2 oz/60 g) butter, melted

FILLING
¹/₄ cup (2 fl oz/60 ml) water
1 tablespoon unflavored gelatin
1 lb (500 g) cream cheese
¹/₂ cup (4 oz/125 g) sugar
¹/₂ cup (4 fl oz/125 ml) milk
¹/₃ cup (3 fl oz/90 ml) cream
4 oz (125 g) semisweet (dark)
chocolate, melted
4 oz (125 g) white chocolate, melted
1 cup (8 fl oz/250 ml) cream, whipped

CHOCOLATE SWIRLS
3¹/₂ oz (100 g) semisweet (dark) chocolate
Heavy (double) cream, for serving

Line a 9-inch (23-cm) spring-form pan with aluminum foil and grease well.

Base: In a food processor, process the cookies (biscuits) until fine. Stir in the butter, then press the mixture into the base of the prepared pan. Refrigerate until firm, 20–30 minutes.

Filling: Place the water in a large cup and sprinkle with the gelatin. Transfer to a saucepan and heat until the gelatin is dissolved and clear. Allow the gelatin to cool slightly.

Beat the cream cheese until smooth, add the sugar and again beat until smooth. Gradually add the milk and cream, beating constantly, until smooth. Fold the gelatin mixture into the cheese mixture. Divide the mixture in half, stir the semisweet (dark) chocolate into one half and the white chocolate into the other half. Fold the whipped cream evenly into both mixtures.

Spread half of the white chocolate mixture onto the base. Freeze for 10 minutes, or until just set. Spread half of the semi-sweet (dark) chocolate mixture carefully over the set white chocolate mixture. Freeze for 10 minutes, or until just set. Repeat, using the remainder of the mixtures. Refrigerate for 3 hours, or overnight, until set.

Chocolate Swirls: Melt the chocolate and place in a pastry (piping) bag fitted with a fine plain nozzle. Pipe swirls onto a sheet of parchment or waxed (greaseproof) paper and refrigerate until set, about 30 minutes.

Decorate the top of the cake with the chocolate swirls. Serve the cake immediately with the cream.

CHERRY FOREST CAKE

Serves 10–12

CAKE
³/₄ cup (3 oz/90 g) unsweetened
cocoa powder
1¹/₂ cups (12 fl oz/375 ml) boiling water
3 eggs
1 teaspoon vanilla extract (essence)
2¹/₂ cups (10 oz/315 g) self-rising flour
2 cups (12 oz/375 g) packed brown sugar
1¹/₂ teaspoons baking soda
(bicarbonate of soda)
Pinch salt
1 cup (8 oz/250 g) sweet (unsalted) butter

GANACHE
11 oz (345 g) semisweet (dark) chocolate
²/₃ cup (5 oz/155 g) sweet (unsalted) butter

SUGAR-COATED CHERRIES
2²/₃ cups (1 lb/500 g) fresh cherries
2 egg whites
³/₄ cup (6 oz/185 g) sugar
Edible flowers, to decorate

Preheat the oven to 350°F (180°C/Gas 4). Butter two 8-inch (20-cm) round cake pans and line with some baking parchment or waxed (greaseproof) paper.
Cake: In a bowl, combine the cocoa and the water and whisk until smooth. In a separate bowl combine the eggs, the vanilla, and one-fourth of the cocoa mixture; set aside. In a large mixing bowl combine all of the dry ingredients, add the butter and the

remaining three-quarters of the cocoa mixture and beat until well combined. Gradually beat in the egg and cocoa mixture, until combined and smooth. Pour the mixture into the prepared pans and bake for 30–35 minutes, or until a skewer inserted in the middle of each cake comes out clean. Allow each cake to cool for 10 minutes in the pan before turning out onto a wire rack to cool completely.

Ganache: Combine the chocolate and butter in the top of a double boiler. Stir over low heat until melted and combined. Divide the mixture evenly between two bowls. Refrigerate one batch for 10–15 minutes, or until just set. Remove from the refrigerator and whisk until lighter in color, 2–3 minutes. Spread half of the chilled ganache over one cake layer, top with the other half and cover with the remaining ganache. Using a small metal spatula, make swirl marks in the ganache to resemble bark. Pour the unrefrigerated ganache over the assembled cake, taking care not to cover all of the bottom ganache layer.

Sugar-coated Cherries: Wash the cherries and pat them dry. Lightly whisk the egg whites and place in a shallow bowl. Place the sugar in another shallow bowl or plate. Dip each cherry into the egg white, allow the excess to drip off, and then roll in the sugar. Place the cherries onto a wire rack covered with a sheet of baking parchment or waxed (greaseproof) paper until the sugar has set, about 5 minutes.

Decorate the top of the cake with the sugar-coated cherries and edible flowers.

*LEFT AND
OPPOSITE:
Cherry Forest Cake*

STRAWBERRY VACHERIN
Serves 8–10

MOUSSE
3 cups (1½ lb/750 g) strawberries
1 cup (7 oz/220 g) sugar
2 tablespoons lemon juice
2 tablespoons unflavored gelatin
¾ cup (6 fl oz/185 ml) hot water
1¼ cups (10 fl oz/315 ml) cream, whipped

MERINGUE
8 egg whites
Pinch of cream of tartar
1 cup (8 oz/250 g) superfine (caster) sugar
1½ cups (8 oz/250 g) confectioners' (icing) sugar
Whipped cream, to decorate
2 cups (1 lb/500 g) strawberries, to decorate

Lightly grease an 8-cup (2-qt/2-l) charlotte mold with grapeseed oil.

Mousse: Combine the strawberries, sugar, and lemon juice in a processor and process until smooth. Sprinkle the gelatin over the water and let dissolve, about 5 minutes. Stir through the strawberry mixture and refrigerate until the mixture begins to set, about 30 minutes. Lightly fold in the whipped cream and pour into the charlotte mold. Refrigerate until set, about 40 minutes.

Meringue: Preheat the oven to 225°F (110°C/ Gas ¼). Line two baking sheets with parchment or waxed (greaseproof) paper.

Beat the egg whites and cream of tartar until soft peaks form. Gradually beat in 4 tablespoons of the superfine (caster) sugar and continue beating for 2–3 minutes. Add the remaining 5½ oz (170 g) of sugar and all of the confectioners' (icing) sugar and fold through quickly and lightly with a metal spoon.

Place the meringue in a pastry (piping) bag with a plain nozzle and pipe finger-shaped lengths ½– ¾ inch (1–2 cm) higher than the mousse onto the baking sheets. Bake for 1 hour, or until meringues sound hollow when gently tapped. Turn off the oven. Loosen the meringues and leave in the oven for a further 30 minutes, until dry.

STRAWBERRY VACHERIN

1. Combine the strawberries, sugar, and the lemon juice in a food processor and process until smooth.

2. Sprinkle the gelatin over the water, to dissolve. Stir through the berries and refrigerate until beginning to thicken.

3. Lightly fold in the whipped cream.

4. Pour into a charlotte mold and refrigerate until set.

OPPOSITE: Strawberry Vacherin

Loosen the edges of the mousse with a knife that has been dipped in hot water. Turn out onto a serving plate and slide rapidly from side to side to unmold the mousse. If necessary, dip the mold briefly into a bowl of hot water and repeat the procedure until the mousse is unmolded.

Spread the cream around the sides of the mousse and place the fingers of meringue over the cream. Pile the strawberries on top of the mousse and serve immediately.

Health & Special Diets

•

Yes, you can have your cake and eat it with a clear conscience
with these life-enhancing recipes which use wholesome
ingredients and healthy substitutions to produce low-fat,
low-calorie treats that don't taste of deprivation at all.

SUGAR-FREE MISO & RAISIN CAKE
Serves 10–12

2 cups (12 oz/375 g)
golden raisins (sultanas)
1 vanilla bean, split
¼ teaspoon salt
1 teaspoon lotus root
tea powder, optional
1 teaspoon freshly grated ginger
3 cups (24 fl oz/750 ml) water
1 tablespoon rice or barley miso
2 tablespoons corn oil
1 tablespoon baking powder
½ cup (4 fl oz/125 ml) pear concentrate
3 cups (12 oz/375 g)
whole wheat (wholemeal) flour
½ cup (2 oz/60 g) ground almonds,
for serving

Preheat the oven to 350°F (180°C/Gas 4). Oil and line a 9-inch (23-cm) round cake pan.

Combine the golden raisins (sultanas), vanilla bean, salt, lotus root tea powder, and ginger in a saucepan with the water. Bring to a boil, then reduce the heat and simmer for 15 minutes, or until the golden raisins (sultanas) are plump. Add the miso and oil and set aside to cool, about 20 minutes. Transfer the mixture to a bowl and add the remaining ingredients, stirring until combined. Pour into the prepared pan. Bake for 40–45 minutes, or until a skewer inserted in the middle of the cake comes out clean. Allow the cake to cool in the pan for 10 minutes before turning out onto a wire rack to cool completely.

Sprinkle with ground almonds and serve.

PEACH UPSIDE-DOWN CAKE
Serves 8–10

⅔ cup (5 fl oz/155 ml) grapeseed oil
¼ cup (2 fl oz/60 ml) pear concentrate
5–6 medium peaches or nectarines,
halved and pitted
2 eggs
1 teaspoon vanilla extract (essence)
2 cups (16 fl oz/500 ml) still apple cider
2½ cups (10 oz/315 g) stoneground
whole wheat (wholemeal) flour, sifted
½ teaspoon ground cinnamon
½ teaspoon ground ginger
¾ cup (3 oz/90 g) roasted chopped
macadamia nuts
Grated zest (rind) of 1 orange

Preheat oven to 350°F (180°C/Gas 4). Butter and flour a 9-inch (23-cm) round springform cake pan. In a saucepan heat 2 tablespoons of the oil, and the pear concentrate. Add the halved peaches or nectarines and cook for 5–6 minutes, or until just tender. Set aside for 20 minutes, or until cool. Beat the eggs until fluffy, 2–3 minutes. Gradually add the remaining ½ cup (4 fl oz/125 ml) oil, and the vanilla. Stir in the remaining ingredients. Drain the fruit, place it decoratively around the base of the pan and pour the batter over it. Bake for 30–35 minutes, or until a skewer inserted in the middle of the cake comes out clean. Cool in the pan for at least 10 minutes before turning out onto a platter to serve.

PREVIOUS PAGES: Sugar-free Miso & Raisin Cake
OPPOSITE AND ABOVE : Peach Upside-down Cake

COCONUT & ALMOND MACAROONS
Makes 20–25

4 egg whites
¹/₄ teaspoon salt
1 teaspoon lemon juice
¹/₄ cup (2 fl oz/60 ml) pear concentrate
¹/₂ teaspoon ground cinnamon
¹/₂ cup (1¹/₂ oz/45 g) flaked
(desiccated) coconut
1 cup (3¹/₂ oz/100 g) roasted
and ground almonds
¹/₂ cup (3 oz/90 g) arrowroot flour
1 teaspoon grated lemon zest (rind)
1 teaspoon vanilla extract (essence)

Preheat the oven to 375°F (190°C/Gas 5). Line a baking sheet with baking parchment or waxed (greaseproof) paper and lightly grease the paper. Using an electric mixer, beat the egg whites with the salt until stiff peaks form. Combine the lemon juice and pear concentrate and gradually beat into the egg whites. Fold in the combined dry ingredients, lemon zest (rind), and vanilla. Drop teaspoonfuls of the mixture onto the prepared sheet, about ³/₄ inch (2 cm) apart. Bake for 10–15 minutes, or until light golden in color and almost firm to the touch. Cool on a wire rack completely before serving

Coconut & Almond Macaroons

PRUNE, NUT & SEED CAKE

Serves 8–10

3 eggs
²⁄₃ cup (5 oz/155 g) sugar
¹⁄₂ cup (2 oz/60 g) chopped pecans
¹⁄₂ cup (2 oz/60 g) chopped,
roasted hazelnuts
¹⁄₂ cup (2 oz/60 g) chopped
blanched almonds
2 tablespoons sunflower seeds,
roughly chopped
2 tablespoons pepitas,
roughly chopped
2 oz (60 g) carob or semisweet (dark)
chocolate, roughly chopped
²⁄₃ cup (4 oz/125 g)
chopped pitted prunes

1¹⁄₃ cups (5¹⁄₂ oz/170 g) self-rising
flour, sifted
1 tablespoon (¹⁄₂ oz/15 g) butter, melted

Preheat the oven to 350°F (180°C/Gas 4). Lightly grease an 8-inch (20-cm) round cake pan and line the base with baking parchment or waxed (greaseproof) paper.

Beat the eggs and sugar with an electric mixer for about 5 minutes, or until the mixture is thick and pale. Stir in the nuts, seeds, carob or chocolate, and prunes. Fold the flour gently into the mixture in 2 batches. Quickly fold in the butter and stir just until combined. Spread into the prepared pan. Bake for 40 minutes, or until a skewer inserted in the middle of the cake comes out clean. Cool in the pan for 10 minutes before turning out onto a wire rack to cool completely. Cut the cake into thin slices and serve.

PRUNE, NUT & SEED CAKE

1. Beat the eggs and sugar for 5 minutes until the mixture is thick and pale.

3. Fold the flour gently into the mixture in 2 batches.

2. Fold in the nuts, seeds, carob, and prunes.

4. Quickly fold in the butter and stir until just combined.

OPPOSITE: Prune, Nut & Seed Cake

LEMON & MANGO CAKE WITH CRUNCHY ALMOND TOPPING
Serves 8–10

1 cup (3¹/₂ oz/100 g) ground almonds
1 cup (4 oz/125 g) rice
flour, sifted
1 cup (4 oz/125 g) cornstarch
(cornflour), sifted
¹/₂ cup (4 fl oz/125 ml) grapeseed oil
¹/₂ cup (4 fl oz/125 ml) concentrated
apple juice
2 lemons, unpeeled and puréed
1 teaspoon vanilla extract (essence)
¹/₄ teaspoon salt
3 teaspoons baking powder
1 cup (8 fl oz/250 ml) unsweetened
apple juice

TOPPING
2 tablespoons grapeseed oil
1 large mango, or 13¹/₂ oz (425 g) canned
mango, drained, sliced, and chopped into
¹/₂-inch (1-cm) cubes
¹/₂ cup (2 oz/60 g) chopped,
roasted almonds
¹/₂ cup (3 oz/90 g) currants or golden
raisins (sultanas)
1 teaspoon ground ginger
1 teaspoon ground cinnamon

Preheat the oven to 350°F (180°C/Gas 4). Grease a 9-inch (23-cm) square cake pan and lightly dust with flour.

In a large bowl, combine the ground almonds, rice flour, and cornstarch (cornflour). In the bowl of a food processor, combine the oil, apple juice, and puréed lemons. Process until smooth, then fold into the flour mixture. Add all of the remaining ingredients and stir until combined. Pour into the prepared pan. Bake for 30–40 minutes, or until the cake comes away from the sides of the pan and a skewer inserted in the center of the cake comes out clean. Allow to cool

in the pan for 10 minutes before turning out onto a wire rack to cool completely.

Topping: In a saucepan, combine all of the ingredients. Gently stir over medium heat for 5–7 minutes, or until the topping bubbles. Spoon the warm topping over the cake and serve.

●

STAINED GLASS LOAF
Serves 10

25 dried apricot halves
8 dried figs, halved
8 prunes, whole
5 dried peaches, halved
5 dried pears, halved
1 cup (8 fl oz/250 ml) water
1 cup (8 fl oz/250 ml)
unsweetened apple juice
1 large banana, peeled
1 cup (4 oz/125 g) whole wheat
(wholemeal) self-rising flour
¹/₂ cup (2 oz/60 g) finely ground almonds
¹/₄ teaspoon ground cinnamon
1 teaspoon grated orange zest (rind)

Preheat the oven to 350°F (180°C/Gas 4). Butter an 8 x 4-inch (20 x 10-cm) loaf pan.

Place all of the dried fruit in a saucepan, add the water and apple juice, cover and simmer for 10 minutes. Drain the cooking liquid from the fruit into the bowl of a food processor. Add 10 of the cooked apricots and the banana and process until smooth. Add the flour, almonds, cinnamon, and orange (zest) rind and process until combined and the mixture is smooth. Stir in the remaining fruit. Spoon the mixture into the prepared pan. Bake for 40–45 minutes, or until a skewer inserted in the middle of the cake comes out clean. Allow the cake to cool in the pan before turning out onto a wire rack to cool completely. Serve cut in slices.

OPPOSITE: Lemon & Mango Cake with Crunchy Almond Topping

BLUEBERRY BRAN MUFFINS
Makes 12

1 cup (4 oz/125 g) processed bran
1 cup (8 fl oz/250 ml) skim milk
½ cup (4 oz/125 g) butter,
at room temperature
1 cup (6 oz/185 g) lightly packed
brown sugar
1 egg
2 cups (8 oz/250 g) whole wheat
(wholemeal) self-rising flour
1 cup (8 oz/250 g)
fresh or frozen blueberries

Preheat the oven to 375°F (190°C/Gas 5). Butter a 12-cup muffin pan.

Soak the bran in the milk for approximately 30 minutes, or until all of the liquid is absorbed. Cream the butter and sugar until light and fluffy. Beat in the egg. Add the bran mixture, then fold in the flour and mix well. Stir in the blueberries and spoon the mixture into the prepared muffin pan. Bake for 25–30 minutes, or until risen and quite golden and a skewer inserted in the middle of a muffin comes out clean. Cool in the pan for 5 minutes before turning out onto a wire rack to cool completely.

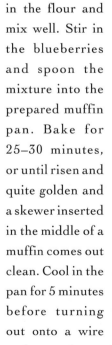

Serve warm or cool with a low-fat spread.

PREVIOUS PAGES: Stained Glass Loaf (left) and
Blueberry Bran Muffins (right)
OPPOSITE AND ABOVE: Fresh Fruit Almond Cake

FRESH FRUIT ALMOND CAKE
Serves 10–12

3 eggs
1 cup (8 oz/250 g) sugar or
¾ cup (6 fl oz/185 ml) pear concentrate
1 teaspoon vanilla extract (essence)
1½ cups (6 oz/185 g) stoneground
all-purpose (plain) flour
2 teaspoons baking powder
1 cup (5 oz/155 g) ground almonds
½ cup (4 fl oz/125 ml) milk or
apple juice
½ cup (4 oz/125 g) vegetable shortening
or ¾ cup (6 fl oz/185 ml) grapeseed oil
3 firm ripe plums, halved and pitted
3 firm ripe apricots, halved and pitted
Extra ground almonds, for serving

Preheat the oven to 350°F (180°C/Gas 4). Butter a 9-inch (23-cm) springform cake pan and line the base with baking parchment or waxed (greaseproof) paper.

Place all of the ingredients, except the fruit, in a food processor and process until well combined. Pour the mixture into the prepared pan and decoratively place the fruit, cut-sides down, around the top. Bake for 40–50 minutes, or until a skewer inserted in the middle of the cake comes out clean. Cool the cake in the pan before removing the sides.

Sprinkle the top of the cake with a little of the extra ground almonds and serve.

Fantasy

•

Satisfy your creative self and impress your friends and family with these inspired delectables. The basic recipes and assembly are easy to follow, the only limit to the finishing flourishes is your imagination!

SOMBRERO
Serves 15–20

12 eggs
2 cups (16 oz/500 g) sugar
3 cups (12 oz/375 g) all-purpose (plain) flour
1 teaspoon baking powder
1½ cups (12 oz/375 g) butter
Grated zest (rind) of 2 limes

ICING
1 cup (8 oz/250 g) butter, softened
1 cup (6 oz/185 g) confectioners'
(icing) sugar, sifted
Liquorice, jellies, candies

Preheat the oven to 350°F (180°C/Gas 4). Butter two 12 x 9-inch (30 x 23-cm) rectangular cake pans, and a 4-cup (1-qt/1-l) capacity pudding basin or a Dolly Varden cake pan.
Beat the eggs and sugar until pale and thick, 7–10 minutes. Fold in the combined flour and baking powder in 3 batches, adding the butter and lime zest (rind) with the last batch. Pour equal amounts of the batter into the rectangular pans and fill the pudding basin with the remainder so that it is three-fourths full. Bake the rectangular cakes for 20–25 minutes, or until firm to the touch in the center. Bake the pudding-shaped cake for 25–30 minutes, or until firm to the touch. Cool in the pan for 2–3 minutes before turning out onto a wire rack to cool completely. Place the 2 rectangular cakes alongside each other, with the 12-inch (30-cm) edges together. Cut into the shape of a circle. Trim the off-cuts into small semi-circles and place on opposite sides of the circle to form the rim of the hat. Place the pudding-shaped cake flat-side down in the center of the circle.
Icing: In a large bowl, beat the butter until soft and pale, 3–4 minutes. Gradually add the sugar and beat until smooth, about 2–3 minutes.
Spread the assembled cake with the icing and decorate with the candies so that they resemble the intricate patterns of a sombrero. Serve.

HEART CAKE
Serves 8

4 eggs
½ cup (4 oz/125 g) sugar
1 cup (4 oz/125 g) all-purpose (plain) flour
¼ cup (2 oz/60 g) butter, melted
1 teaspoon vanilla extract (essence)
1 drop red food coloring

ICING
1½ cups (8 oz/250 g) confectioners'
(icing) sugar
1 egg white, lightly whisked
1 teaspoon raspberry extract (essence)
2 drops red food coloring

Preheat the oven to 350°F (180°C/Gas 4). Butter and flour a medium-sized heart-shaped cake pan. Beat together the eggs and sugar until pale and the mixture forms ribbons, about 3–4 minutes. Sift the flour into the batter in 3 batches, folding in after each addition. Add the butter, vanilla, and food coloring with the last batch. Pour the batter into the prepared pan. Bake for 20–30 minutes, or until a skewer inserted in the center of the cake comes out clean. Let cool in the pan for 2–3 minutes before turning out onto a wire rack to cool completely.
Icing: Sift the sugar into a large bowl. Gradually stir in the combined egg white and raspberry extract (essence) until smooth, about 1–2 minutes. Reserve 2 tablespoons of the icing for decoration and color the rest with 1 drop of the red food coloring. Color the reserved icing with the remaining drop of food coloring so that it is darker. Spread a thin layer of the paler icing evenly over the cake and allow it to set. Fill a pastry (piping) bag with the reserved icing and pipe small decorative dots and a fine rim around the top edge of the cake. Decorate with rose petals if desired and serve.

OPPOSITE: Heart Cake
PREVIOUS PAGES: Sombrero

FLORAL BOMBE
Serves 10

³/₄ cup (6 oz/185 g) sweet (unsalted) butter
³/₄ cup (6 oz/185 g) sugar
3 eggs
³/₄ cup (4 oz/125 g) fine semolina flour
¹/₂ cup (2 oz/60 g) all-purpose
(plain) flour, sifted
2 teaspoons baking powder
Grated zest (rind) of 1 orange
Grated zest (rind) of ¹/₂ lemon

ICING
1 cup (8 oz/250 g) sweet (unsalted)
butter, at room temperature
1 cup (6 oz/185 g)
confectioners' (icing) sugar, sifted
2 teaspoons orange flower water
Small cake decorators' flowers
or nasturtiums and violets

OPPOSITE: Floral Bombe

Preheat the oven to 350°F (180°C/Gas 4). Butter a 4-cup (2-qt/2-l) capacity pudding basin or Dolly Varden cake pan.

Cream the butter and sugar until light and fluffy, 3–4 minutes. Add the eggs, one at a time, beating well after each addition. Fold in the semolina, flour, baking powder, and orange and lemon zest (rind). Pour the batter into the prepared pan. Bake for 50–60 minutes, or until a skewer inserted in the middle of the cake comes out clean. Let cool in the pan for 10 minutes before turning out onto a wire rack to cool completely.

When the cake is cool, even off the base by cutting away any peaks that may have formed.

Icing: Beat the butter until pale, 3–4 minutes. Gradually add the sugar, beating until smooth, 2–3 minutes. Add the orange flower water and beat to combine thoroughly, about 30 seconds. Place the cake, base down, on a serving plate. Using a large metal spatula, cover the cake with the icing. Using a smaller spatula, create small peaks and ridges in the icing. Decorate the cake with the flowers, cut into wedges and serve.

FLORAL BOMBE

1. Cream the butter and sugar until soft and pale.

3. Place the cake base down and, using a large metal spatula, cover the cake with icing.

2. Gradually add the confectioners' (icing) sugar.

4. Using a smaller spatula, create small peaks and valleys.

WHITE CHOCOLATE BERRY CAKE

Serves 10–12

6 egg yolks
1 cup (8 fl oz/250 ml) milk
1 teaspoon vanilla extract (essence)
3¹/₃ cups (13 oz/410 g) self-rising flour
1 cup (8 oz/250 g) sugar
¹/₂ cup (4 oz/125 g) butter, softened
5¹/₂ oz (170 g) white chocolate, melted

FILLING AND TOPPING
9¹/₂ oz (300 g) white chocolate, melted
2 cups (1 lb/500 g) mixed summer berries

Preheat oven to 350°F (180°C/Gas 4). Butter two 9-inch (23-cm) springform pans and line bases with parchment or waxed (greaseproof) paper.

Combine the egg yolks, ¹/₄ cup (2 fl oz/60 ml) of the milk, and the vanilla in a bowl.

In a large bowl, combine the flour and sugar. Add the softened butter and the remaining ³/₄ cup (6 fl oz/185 ml) milk. Beat on low speed to combine, 3–4 minutes. Gradually add the egg mixture in 3 batches, beating well after each addition. Add the melted chocolate and beat to combine, about 2 minutes. Pour the mixture into the prepared pans. Bake for 35–40 minutes, or until a skewer inserted in the center of each cake comes out clean. Let cool in the pan for 10 minutes before turning out onto a wire rack to cool completely.

Filling and Topping: Spread one-third of the warm melted chocolate over 1 cake layer using a large metal spatula.

Place the berries, reserving a few for decoration, on top of the cake layer spread with the chocolate. Place the second cake layer on top and cover the assembled cake with the remaining melted white chocolate. Decorate with the reserved berries and serve.

BELOW AND RIGHT: White Chocolate Berry Cake

CHOCOLATE CHECKERBOARD CAKE
Serves 10

1 cup (8 oz/250 g) butter
1 cup (8 oz/250 g) sugar
4 eggs
1¹/₂ cups (6 oz/185 g) self-rising flour
2¹/₂ oz (75 g) semisweet
(dark) chocolate, melted

PEPPERMINT CREAM
¹/₂ cup (4 oz/125 g) butter
2 oz (60 g) cream cheese
3¹/₃ cups (1¹/₃ lb/615 g)
confectioners' (icing) sugar, sifted
1 tablespoon milk
1 drop peppermint extract (essence)

CHOCOLATE COATING
6¹/₂ oz (200g) bittersweet (dark)
chocolate, chopped
1 tablespoon grapeseed oil

Preheat the oven to 350°F (180°C/Gas 4). Butter two 8 x 4-inch (20 x 10-cm) loaf pans and line with parchment or waxed (greaseproof) paper. Cream the butter and sugar until light and fluffy, about 2–3 minutes. Add the eggs, one at a time, beating well after each addition. Fold in the flour, mixing until smooth. Divide the batter into 2 portions. Fold the chocolate into 1 portion, mixing until well combined.

Spread the chocolate batter into one of the prepared pans and the plain batter into the remaining pan. Bake in the oven for 45 minutes, or untila skewer inserted in the center comes out clean. Let stand for 5 minutes before turning out onto a wire rack to cool completely. The cakes may be made a day ahead for easy cutting.

Trim the cakes to remove the dark tops and sides. Cut each cake in half horizontally, then each half into 3 lengths so that there are 6 lengths per cake.

Peppermint Cream: Beat together the butter and cream cheese until light and creamy, about 2–3 minutes. Add the sugar a little at a time, beating until smooth. Beat in the milk and peppermint until smooth.

To form the first layer, alternately join 2 chocolate lengths with 2 plain lengths using the peppermint cream. Cover with one-third of the remaining peppermint cream. For the second layer ensure that the chocolate lengths are topped by plain lengths and plain lengths are topped by chocolate lengths to achieve a checkerboard effect. Join each length with peppermint cream and cover with another third of peppermint cream. Repeat for the third layer joining the cake lengths with the remaining peppermint cream. Cover with plastic wrap and refrigerate until firm, about 30 minutes.

Chocolate Coating: In the top of a double boiler, melt the chocolate over low heat. Add the oil and stir until smooth. Allow the coating to cool slightly before spreading over the top and sides of the cake using a large metal spatula. Serve.

MARBLE CAKE
Serves 10

3/4 cup (6 oz/185 g) butter
1 1/2 cups (12 oz/375 g) sugar
1 1/2 teaspoons vanilla extract (essence)
3 eggs
2 cups (8 oz/250 g) self-rising flour
Pinch salt
3/4 cup (6 fl oz/185 ml) milk
1 drop red food coloring
1 drop red and 1 drop blue
food coloring, combined
1 drop green food coloring
1 drop yellow and 1 drop red
food coloring, combined

ICING
1/2 cup (4 oz/125 g) butter
2 1/2 cups (14 oz/440 g) confectioners'
(icing) sugar, sifted
Ribbon, for decorating

Preheat the oven to 350°F (180°C/Gas 4). Butter a 9 x 5-inch (23 x 12-cm) loaf pan.
Cream the butter, sugar, and vanilla until light and fluffy, about 2–3 minutes. Add the eggs, one at a time, beating well after each addition. Fold in the flour and salt in 3 batches alternately with the milk, starting and finishing with the flour.
Divide the mixture into 5 equal portions. Leaving 1 portion uncolored, tint the remaining 4 portions pink, mauve, pale green, and apricot.

Drop alternating spoonfuls of each portion into the prepared pan until all the mixture is used. Bake for 50 minutes, or until a skewer inserted in the middle of the cake comes out clean. Cool the cake in the pan for 10 minutes before turning out onto a wire rack to cool completely.
Icing: Beat the butter until smooth, about 2–3 minutes. Add the sugar, 1/2 cup (3 oz/90 g) at a time, mixing until smooth. If the icing is too soft to use, refrigerate until firm, about 10–15 minutes. When the cake is cool, cover with the icing and tie decoratively with the ribbon.

•

STARRY NIGHT CAKE
Serves 8

1/2 cup (4 oz/125 g) butter
1 cup (8 oz/250 g) sugar
3 eggs
1 1/4 cups (5 oz/155 g) all-purpose
(plain) flour
1/3 cup (3 fl oz/90 ml) sour cream
1 teaspoon vanilla extract (essence)

ICING
1 1/2 cups (8 oz/250 g)
confectioners' (icing) sugar
1 egg white, lightly whisked
1 drop each red, green, blue, and
black food coloring
Confectioners' (icing) sugar, for dusting

Preheat the oven to 350°F (180°C/Gas 4). Butter a 9 x 10-inch (23 x 25-cm) star-shaped or a 9-inch (23-cm) round cake pan.

Cream the butter and sugar until it is light and fluffy, 2–3 minutes. Add the eggs, one at a time, beating well after each addition. Fold in the flour in 3 batches alternately with the sour cream and vanilla. Pour the batter into the prepared pan. Bake for 50–60 minutes, or until a skewer inserted in the center of the cake comes out clean. Let the cake cool in the pan for 10 minutes before turning out onto a wire rack to cool completely.

Icing: Sift the sugar into a large bowl. Gradually stir in the egg white, mixing until smooth, about 1 minute. Divide the icing evenly between 4 separate bowls and add a different food color to each. Using a warmed metal spatula, spread the points of the star with the red, green, and blue icings. Using a pastry (piping) bag, pipe black icing around the edges of the colors. Dust the center of the cake with the sugar and serve.

PREVIOUS PAGES: Chocolate Checkerboard Cake (left) and Marble Cake (right)
ABOVE AND LEFT: Starry Night Cake

ARTIST'S PALETTE
Serves 20

8 eggs
1¹/₃ cups (10 oz/315 g) sugar
2 cups (8 oz/250 g) all-purpose (plain) flour
2 teaspoons baking powder
1 cup (8 oz/250 g) butter, melted

ICING
3 cups (1 lb/500 g) confectioners' (icing) sugar
¹/₄ cup (2 fl oz/60 ml) water
1 drop red food coloring
2 drops red, green, and blue food coloring
1 drop red and 1 drop blue
food coloring, combined
2 drops black food coloring

Preheat oven to 350°F (180°C/Gas 4). Butter two 12 x 9-inch (30 x 23-cm) rectangular cake pans. Beat the eggs and sugar until thick and pale, about 5 minutes. Fold in the combined flour and baking powder in 2 batches, adding the butter with the last batch. Divide the batter evenly between the pans. Bake for 20 minutes, or until the cakes are firm to the touch in the center. Cool the cakes in the pan for 2–3 minutes before turning out onto a wire rack to cool completely. Place the cakes alongside each other with the 12-inch (30-cm) edges together. Cut out the shape of an artist's palette using a serrated knife. **Icing:** Sift the sugar into a bowl. Gradually add the water, stirring until the icing is smooth and spreadable. Divide the icing into 2 even batches. Leaving 1¹/₂ cups of the icing white, divide the rest evenly into 6 portions and add a different food color to each, mixing well.

Cover the cake with the plain white icing using a warmed metal spatula. Fill a pastry (piping) bag with one of the colored icings and "paint" blobs on the top of the cake. Repeat until all the colors are used and the surface of the cake resembles paint being mixed on an artist's palette. Serve.

Artist's Palette

Traditional

·

Just like Mother used to bake... and with good reason.
Wherever you go in the world there will be a cake
that is as representative of the region as its landmarks.
These recipes also include some time-honored
treats for festive occasions.

ORANGE SYRUP CAKE
Serves 8–10

CAKE
1 cup (8 oz/250 g) sweet (unsalted)
butter, at room temperature
$^3/_4$ cup ($6^1/_2$ oz/200 g) sugar
2 tablespoons finely grated
orange zest (rind)
4 eggs
2 cups (8 oz/250 g) self-rising flour, sifted

SYRUP
1 cup (8 oz/250 g) sugar
Juice of 2 oranges
$^1/_4$ cup (2 fl oz/60 ml) water
Grated zest (rind) of 3 oranges
Heavy (double) cream, for serving

Preheat the oven to 350°F (180°C/Gas 4). Grease a 9-inch (23-cm) round cake pan and line the base with parchment or waxed (greaseproof) paper.
Cake: Cream the butter and sugar until light and fluffy. Beat in the orange zest (rind). Add the eggs, one at a time, beating well after each addition. Fold in the flour. Pour the batter into the prepared pan. Bake for 40–50 minutes, or until a skewer inserted in the middle of the cake comes out clean. Allow the cake to cool in the pan for 10 minutes.
Syrup: In a saucepan, combine all of the ingredients except the zest and stir over low heat to dissolve the sugar. Add the zest and bring to a boil. Boil for 5–7 minutes, or until the zest is transparent and the syrup is slightly thickened and reduced by one-third. Strain the syrup, reserving the zest for decoration.
While the cake is still warm, make 15–20 holes about $^1/_2$ inch (1 cm) apart in the top using a skewer. Brush with the syrup, making sure it is directed into the holes. Decorate the cake with the reserved zest and serve warm or cool with the cream.

PREVIOUS PAGES: Orange Syrup Cake
OPPOSITE: Panettone

PANETTONE
Serves 12

1 cup (5 oz/155 g) golden raisins (sultanas)
$^1/_4$ cup ($1^1/_2$ oz/45 g) glacéed red cherries
$^1/_4$ cup ($1^1/_2$ oz/45 g) glacéed green cherries
$^1/_3$ cup (3 oz/90 g) mixed candied citrus peel
$^1/_4$ cup ($1^1/_2$ oz/45 g) glacéed pineapple
1 teaspoon ground allspice
$^1/_2$ cup (4 fl oz/125 ml) Grand Marnier

DOUGH
$^1/_2$ oz (15 g) fresh yeast
2 tablespoons warm milk
$4^3/_4$ cups ($1^1/_4$ lb/600 g) all-purpose
(plain) flour
$^1/_3$ cup (3 oz/90 g) sugar
$^1/_2$ teaspoon salt
3 whole eggs, plus 3 egg yolks
1 cup (8 oz/250 g) sweet (unsalted)
butter, chopped into pieces and softened

Combine the fruit, allspice, and Grand Marnier in a bowl and let stand for 24 hours, stirring occasionally.
Dough: Crumble the yeast over the milk and whisk to dissolve. Let stand for 10 minutes, or until frothy. In a large bowl, combine the flour, sugar, and salt. Beat in the eggs and egg yolks, one at a time, until combined. The mixture will appear lumpy. Add the yeast mixture and softened butter. Beat until the mixture comes away from the side of the bowl and sticks to the beaters. Cover with a damp tea towel and refrigerate for 4 hours, or until doubled in bulk. Punch the dough down and gently knead in the fruit mixture. Return to the bowl, cover with a damp tea towel and refrigerate for 24 hours.
Preheat the oven to 400°F (200°C/Gas 6). Lightly grease an 8-cup (2-qt/2-l) charlotte mold and line the base and at least 4 inches (10 cm) of the sides with parchment or waxed (greaseproof) paper.
Place the dough in the mold and rest in a warm place until doubled in size, about $1^1/_2$ hours.
Bake for 40–50 minutes, or until the top sounds hollow when tapped. Let cool completely before turning out to serve.

GINGERBREAD

Serves 8–10

1²/₃ cups (13 fl oz/410 ml) light corn
syrup (golden syrup)
¹/₃ cup (4 fl oz/125 ml) honey
³/₄ cup (6 fl oz/185 ml) grapeseed oil
1 cup (8 fl oz/250 ml) water
1 cup (6 oz/185 g) packed brown sugar
3 eggs
2 cups (8 oz/250 g)
all-purpose (plain) flour
1 cup (4 oz/125 g) self-rising flour
1 teaspoon ground allspice
¹/₂ teaspoon ground cinnamon
1 teaspoon ground ginger
¹/₂ teaspoon baking soda
(bicarbonate of soda)

LEMON ICING
Juice of ¹/₂ lemon
1 tablespoon plus 1 teaspoon
(³/₄ oz/20 g) butter, softened
1¹/₄ cups (7 oz/220 g) confectioners'
(icing) sugar

Preheat the oven to 350°F (180°C/Gas 4). Lightly grease an 8-inch (20-cm) square cake pan and line with baking parchment or waxed (greaseproof) paper.

Combine the syrup, honey, oil, water, and sugar in a saucepan. Stir over low heat until the sugar is dissolved, then bring to a boil. Remove from the heat and allow to cool. Add the eggs, one at a time, and mix until smooth. Fold in the flours, spices, and baking soda (bicarbonate of soda), mixing until smooth.

Pour the mixture into the prepared pan. Bake for 1¹/₄ hours, or until a skewer inserted in the center of the cake comes out clean. Let the cake rest in the pan for 10 minutes before turning out onto a wire rack to cool.

Lemon Icing: Combine the lemon juice and butter in the top of a double boiler. Mix until the butter is melted and the mixture smooth. Stir the butter mixture into the sugar, mixing until smooth. Stand the icing over hot water to thin slightly, then spread over the cooled cake as quickly as possible. Serve cut in slices.

OPPOSITE: Gingerbread

GINGERBREAD

1. Combine the syrup, honey, oil, water, and sugar in a pan. Stir over low heat until the sugar is dissolved.

3. Add the eggs, one at a time.

2. Bring to a boil. Remove from heat and allow to cool.

4. Fold in the flours, spice, and soda, mixing until smooth.

IRISH TEACAKE

Serves 10–12

2$\frac{1}{3}$ cups (12 oz/375 g) currants or
golden raisins (sultanas)
1 cup (8 fl oz/250 ml) cold strong tea
1 cup (5 oz/155 g) brown sugar
2 cups (8 oz/250 g) self-rising flour
1 egg
Butter, for serving

In a bowl, combine the currants, tea, and sugar
and leave to soak overnight.

Preheat the oven to 350°F (180°C/Gas 4). Butter a
9 x 4 x 3-inch (23 x 10 x 8-cm) baking pan and line
with parchment or waxed (greaseproof) paper.

Stir the flour and egg into the currant mixture
and pour into the prepared pan. Bake for 1$\frac{1}{2}$
hours, or until a skewer inserted in the middle of
the cake comes out clean. Allow the cake to cool
in the pan for 10 minutes before turning out onto
a wire rack to cool completely.

Serve the cake sliced and spread with butter.

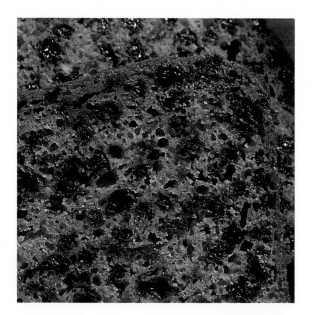

Irish Teacake

DUNDEE FRUIT CAKE
Serves 15

1 cup (8 oz/250 g) sweet
(unsalted) butter
³/₄ cup (6 oz/185 g) sugar
3 eggs
1³/₄ cups (7 oz/220 g) all-purpose
(plain) flour
¹/₂ teaspoon baking powder
Pinch salt
1¹/₃ cups (6¹/₂ oz/200 g)
golden raisins (sultanas)
1¹/₂ cups (7 oz/220 g) currants
³/₄ cup (4 oz/125 g) chopped raisins
²/₃ cup (5 oz/155 g) candied citrus peel
Grated zest (rind) of 1 orange and 1 lemon
²/₃ cup (2¹/₂ oz/75 g) chopped
blanched almonds
1 teaspoon vanilla extract (essence)
and/or almond extract (essence)
2 tablespoons orange juice or sherry
20 blanched whole almonds,
for decoration

Preheat oven to 300°F (150°C/Gas 2). Butter a
9-inch (23-cm) round cake pan and line the base
with parchment or waxed (greaseproof) paper.
Cream the butter and sugar until light and fluffy.
Beat in the eggs, one at a time, beating well after
each addition. Fold in the flour, baking powder,
and salt alternately with the dried fruits, zest
(rind) and chopped almonds. Add the vanilla and/
or almond extract (essence),
and orange juice or sherry. Pour
the mixture into the prepared
pan and decorate with the extra
almonds. Cook for 2 hours, or
until a skewer inserted in the
middle of the cake comes out
clean. Cool completely in the
pan before turning out.

*OPPOSITE AND RIGHT: Dundee
Fruit Cake*

GREEK SEMOLINA & WALNUT CAKE
Serves 15

1 cup (8 oz/250 g) butter
³/₄ cup (6 oz/185 g) sugar
1 teaspoon grated orange zest (rind)
4 eggs, separated
1 cup (4 oz/125 g) all-purpose (plain) flour
1 cup (5 oz/155 g) fine semolina flour
4 teaspoons baking powder
1 teaspoon ground cinnamon
¹/₂ cup (4 fl oz/125 ml) milk
2 cups (8 oz/250 g) coarsely chopped walnuts

SYRUP
1 cup (8 oz/250 g) sugar
1 cup (8 fl oz/250 ml) water
2 whole cloves
2-inch (5-cm) cinnamon stick
1 tablespoon lemon juice
Thin strip of lemon zest (rind)

Preheat the oven to 350°F (180°C/Gas 4). Butter
a 13 x 9 x 2-inch (33 x 23 x 5-cm) baking pan.
Cream the butter, sugar, and orange zest (rind)
until light and fluffy. Add the egg yolks, one at a
time, beating well after each addition. Fold in the
flour, semolina, baking powder, and cinnamon
alternately with the milk. Gently mix in the walnuts. Beat the egg whites until stiff peaks form,
then fold into the mixture. Pour the mixture into
the prepared pan. Bake for 45 minutes, or until a
skewer inserted in the center
comes out clean.

Syrup: Combine the ingredients in a pan. Slowly bring
to a boil, stirring constantly
to dissolve the sugar. Boil
for 10 minutes, remove from
the heat and strain. When
cake is removed from the
oven, pour over the syrup.
Let cool in the pan com-
pletely before turning out.

PEAR & CINNAMON TEACAKE
Serves 8

1 egg, separated
$^1/_2$ cup (4 oz/125 g) sugar
$^1/_2$ cup (4 fl oz/125 ml) milk
$^1/_2$ teaspoon vanilla extract (essence)
$1^1/_2$ tablespoons (1 oz/30 g)
butter, melted
1 cup (4 oz/125 g) self-rising flour, sifted
1 pear, peeled, cored, and thinly sliced

TOPPING
1 tablespoon ($^3/_4$ oz/25 g) butter, melted
$^1/_2$ teaspoon ground cinnamon
1 tablespoon sugar
Heavy (double) cream or butter, for serving

Preheat the oven to 375°F (190°C/Gas 5). Butter an 8-inch (20-cm) round cake pan.

Whisk the egg white until stiff peaks form. Gradually beat in the sugar, then the egg yolk. Stir in the milk, vanilla, and melted butter. Gently fold in the flour, then pour into the prepared pan. Arrange the pear slices on top. Bake for 20–25 minutes, or until a skewer inserted in the middle of the cake comes out clean.

Topping: Allow the cake to cool in the pan for 10 minutes before turning out onto a serving plate. While the cake is still hot, brush the top generously with the melted butter. Combine the cinnamon and sugar and sprinkle over the top. Serve the cake warm or cold with the cream or spread with the butter.

•

SPONGE CAKE WITH LEMON CURD
Serves 8

4 eggs
$^1/_2$ cup (4 oz/125 g) sugar
1 cup (4 oz/125 g) all-purpose (plain) flour

Pinch salt
$^1/_4$ cup (2 oz/60 g) sweet (unsalted)
butter, melted and cooled
Grated zest (rind) of 1 lemon

LEMON CURD (Makes 2 cups)
$^1/_2$ cup (4 oz/125 g) sweet (unsalted) butter
$^2/_3$ cup (5 fl oz/155 ml) lemon juice
1 cup (8 oz/250 g) sugar
3 whole eggs
3 egg yolks
1 cup (8 fl oz/250 ml)
heavy (double) cream, whipped
Confectioners' (icing) sugar, for dusting

Preheat oven to 350°F (180°C/Gas 4). Butter two 8-inch (20-cm) round cake pans and dust with flour. Whisk the eggs and sugar until thick and pale and the mixture forms a ribbon. Fold in the combined flour and salt in 2 batches, adding the butter and lemon zest (rind) with the last batch. Pour the mixture into the prepared pans. Bake for 20–30 minutes, or until the cakes spring back when touched in the center. Allow each cake to cool in the pan for 5 minutes before turning out onto a wire rack to cool completely.

Lemon Curd: In the top of a double boiler, combine the butter, lemon juice, and sugar over a medium heat. Stir until the sugar dissolves and the butter melts. Whisk together the eggs and yolks and gradually pour into the lemon mixture, whisking constantly. Stir over medium heat for 7–10 minutes, or until the curd begins to thicken. Allow to cool completely in the refrigerator to set, about 2 hours.

Spread the top of one cake layer with $^1/_2$ cup (4 fl oz/125 ml) of the lemon curd and the cream, then place the second layer on top. The remaining quantity of lemon curd may be stored in the refrigerator for up to 1 week. Dust the top of the assembled cake with the sugar and serve.

OPPOSITE: Sponge Cake with Lemon Curd
PREVIOUS PAGES: Greek Semolina & Walnut Cake
(left) and Pear & Cinnamon Teacake (right)

STRAWBERRY POUND CAKE
Serves 10–12

**8 oz (250 g) strawberries,
hulled and quartered
2 cups (8 oz/250 g)
all-purpose (plain) flour, sifted
1 cup (8 oz/250 g) sweet (unsalted) butter
1 cup (8 oz/250 g) sugar
4 eggs
Grated zest (rind) of 1 orange
1 teaspoon baking powder**

ICING
**4 oz (125 g) hulled strawberries
1¹/₂ tablespoons
confectioners' (icing) sugar
1¹/₄ cups (10 fl oz/315 ml)
heavy (double) cream, whipped
5–6 extra strawberries, for decoration**

Preheat oven to 350°F (180°C/Gas 4). Butter a 9-inch (23-cm) round cake pan and line the base with parchment or waxed (greaseproof) paper.

Toss the strawberries in a little of the flour, to coat. Cream the butter and sugar until light and fluffy. Beat in the eggs, one at a time, beating well after each addition. Fold in the orange zest (rind), flour, baking powder, and strawberries in 3 batches. Stir to combine after each addition.

Pour the mixture into the prepared pan. Bake for 50 minutes, or until a skewer inserted in the middle of the cake comes out clean.

Cool in the pan for 10 minutes before turning out onto a wire rack to cool completely.

Icing: Place the strawberries and sugar in the bowl of a food processor and process to a purée. Fold into the whipped cream. Ice the cake and decorate with the strawberries and serve.

ABOVE AND OPPOSITE: Strawberry Pound Cake

STRAWBERRY POUND CAKE

1. Toss the strawberries in the flour to coat.

3. Beat in the eggs, one at a time, beating well after each addition.

2. Cream the butter and sugar.

4. Fold in the orange zest, flour, and strawberries in three batches.

Index

ACKNOWLEDGMENTS
Australian Craftworks
Country Floors
Georg Jensen
InMaterial
Royal Copenhagen
Villeroy & Boch
Wardlaw Fabrics